On
Sacred
Time

On Sacred Time

Tapping the Power Within

NICOLE MYERS HENDERSON

TATE PUBLISHING
AND ENTERPRISES, LLC

Published by Tate Publishing & Enterprises, LLC
127 E. Trade Center Terrace | Mustang, Oklahoma 73064 USA
1.888.361.9473 | www.tatepublishing.com

Tate Publishing is committed to excellence in the publishing industry. The company reflects the philosophy established by the founders, based on Psalm 68:11,
"The Lord gave the word and great was the company of those who published it."

Book design copyright © 2014 by Tate Publishing, LLC. All rights reserved.
Cover design by Rtor Maghuyop
Interior design by Jimmy Sevilleno

Published in the United States of America

ISBN: 978-1-63063-278-6
1. Body, Mind & Spirit / General
2. Body, Mind & Spirit / Spiritualism
14.03.28

Dedication

T O THOSE SPECIAL people in my life: I love and value each person that has come and gone including those people and relationships that have been or continue to be a little uncomfortable. We learn from each other, because we are mirror images of one another. You reflect what I need to know about myself and vice versa, as we live, grow, adapt, overcome, and learn to love ourselves and one another more fully.

To my husband, Monty, you are the embodiment of the ultimate warrior. Thank you for your ever-present love and for possessing such a protective disposition. I am happy God brought us together this time around. You have taught me much, and I am grateful for every minute we get to spend sharing this life together. During the toughest of times, we have held it together because of our tenacity and love for one another.

It is to my editor, Tyler Worsham, at Tate Publishing that I owe a debt of gratitude. To be an editor requires special talents that include precision and patience. To my cover designer Rtor Maghuyop and interior designer Jimmy Sevilleno, you both did a fabulous job and I am grateful for your creativity and efforts.

I offer a special thank you to my dear friend, author, and *Spirit Quest* producer Amelia Townsend. We have been friends for a very long time, and it has been my distinct pleasure to not only know you but to have worked with you as well. Thank you for reading over the manuscript. I appreciate your willingness to share your wisdom and insight.

I would also like to thank my mother and father for bringing me into the world. Without the two of you, I would not exist, and I am grateful for the time and energy you had put forth as you nurtured me and my two brothers. I am sure there were many instances where you thought about giving up, and I would not have been one to stand in judgment over you, had you done so. It takes special people to bring children into the world, and I commend you both for willingly, or even unwillingly, participating in God's divine plan, where we all had the opportunity to share this sacred space.

Thank you all for your steadfast support and for sharing your lives with me.

Contents

Preface

A S I BEGIN the painstaking process of reviewing and re-editing this text, I fight with myself over deleting much of the text that the editor suggests is unnecessary. You see, my production manager at Tate sent me the edited material a couple of weeks ago, and I found myself stuck—deadlocked—feeling very anxious about what must go and what I should keep within these pages. To make a decision one way or another, I focused my attention on connecting with my God source, in order to do what was necessary to pull all of this information together for the manuscript's safe return for production. I reflect on why I have chosen to use this text to reveal stories from my life and communicate my experiences in order to awaken something within you—the reader. I willingly chose to remain in a state of allowance, in order to stay connected to a higher authority, perhaps to not allow my own prejudices to overflow onto these pages. I have changed much since I began writing this book more than eight years ago. As you read, please consider that my ideas about God are just that—my ideas—and that I wrote this text so that you would be able to discern for yourself just what resonates for you around your life.

I will take you on a journey through philosophy and religion, Native American prophesy, and into my own hypothesis about how the ebb and flow of our emotions affect the weather, our relationships, and our body. I will describe my hypothesis regarding Cellular Memory, what it is and how I came to understand how matter communicates with all other matter. I will discuss control and manipulation issues, how the ideas of others affect how we live our lives as we try to figure out what is fair and reasonable. Again, much of what I have written about in these pages was created in order to trigger your thought processes, in order to determine what is right for you—to bring you, your body, and your life back into balance—to shift your consciousness from a state of doing into a state of connectedness, allowance, and being.

This book contains many of my own experiences that were revealed to me as I learned how to communicate with the cells of my body. At first it was difficult to let down my guard and share. After all, no one really wants others to sit in judgment over them—myself included. To willfully choose to be vulnerable means that I had to risk ridicule, to remain open to feeling the negativity associated with any emotion you might feel about my experiences and ideas. To fully grasp the complexity of a life of full-blown empathy, you might consider visualizing a spiritual Navy S.E.A.L. of sorts. To allow oneself to *be* empathic means always being vulnerable to outside forces—to walk in someone elses shoes, to risk exposure and condemnation, to lose oneself, and become what someone else is, in order to understand them more fully. You may ask why a reasonable and prudent person would allow this. My only answer is that something moved my soul and told me that there was a need to remind humanity of its connectedness to all things, to each other, and to teach you how to make better use of your thoughts, time, and energy.

Each chapter is designed to teach you something about yourself, to assist you in applying what your body knows at a cellular level, in order to put you back in balance with the world around you. From Indian prophesy about environmental issues, to the maiming and killing of others, to cultural upbringing and societal practices, there is information that will assist you in finding out just what you need to know to restore flow and a sense of stability in your life.

You, the reader, may have gone through some terrible experiences in your life or are going through some now. Your bones and joints may be aching, your spirit may live within a body surrounded by pain, but—by the end of this text—I guarantee that you will know yourself more fully than you ever thought possible. It is my hope that you are able to harvest enough information from my experiences and this text to know the difference between beingness versus the use of power and force, to be open to creating peace in your own life, and willingly helping others do the same.

Remember to treat others as you wish to be treated!
Namaste

Introduction

M Y JOURNEY BEGAN in 1985, after being introduced to a videotaped movie called *Earth Changes*. This documentary expounded upon the Hopi Indian predictions that have continued to affect our planet, and its inhabitants. As with any prophecy, time had to pass in order to see their predictions come to pass. As I actively think about the cataclysmic events that have transpired over the last 20 plus years I feel it safe to conclude that the Hopis had tapped in to a higher power and were able to receive information that would benefit humanity for many, many years. As I consider this I cannot help but wonder if we and the planet would be in better shape had we all been infused with their knowledge from the beginning but to expend any energy on what could have been seems to be more self defeating. I instead feel more compelled to spend this time focusing on how our brothers and sisters will rise again and connect with all things. To reunite with Great Spirit with only pure intention and teach our children the path to peace and oneness-to educate the generations to come, realize that we are not alone and that we are deeply cared for by the source from which we either evolved from or was created by. If you do not have first-hand experience with indian ways, you may have seen movies where the native American could hear messages from the earth, or know what was to come just by paying attention to the animals, wind, water and trees. In keeping with that idea that the Indians were more adept at hearing messages from Great Spirit by way of all living things, we may now be better able to grasp the idea that we all can. We are living and breathing conduits of energy that can willfully expose ourselves to outside forces so that we are able to listen, feel, see, and think more deeply. Knowing that something could happen doesn't mean we live our lives in fear of it, but instead, choose to live in a heightened state of awareness in order to remain open to the information that flows naturally to us—allowing us to protect our planet and our physical forms.

The Hopis predicted many freak accidents and cataclysmic events that have already come to pass; catastrophic events that took loved ones or merely changed the Earth's landscape. People and animals alike have lost their lives. Some might argue that when these events take place, there is nothing we can do. I beg to differ. Conscious awareness changes everything. Predictions of earthquakes, floods, crimes of passion, greed, jealousy and plain acts of stupidity have led us to where we are today- unattached, overloaded and standing on the precipice of collapse. Know that although this may be true, there is a higher power at work here and *it* is inviting us to change, just as it has been since the beginning of time. Everything changes. The Earth is strong but she is constantly adjusting in order to accommodate the load she carries. You can choose to change right along with her—adapting and overcoming—or continue on the path you *think* you should be living, or maybe you will choose to become more aware of your environment and live life as a fully conscious being.

Bad things do happen. Unfortunately, that is the natural cycle of life and death. The world according to the Native American Indians suggested that there must be endings in order to have new beginnings. There is much truth to this.

I have written this book because Great Spirit asked me to share my life with you in an effort to wake you from your long, unconscious slumber. I was told, in 2003, that by sharing my experiences and teaching others, I would help raise universal awareness. They, meaning Spirit—being plural-said that this *time* we were entering into is sacred and that it is imperative that we recognize our own true gifts. This is a very special time! It is a time for change; a time for new beginnings. Mother earth is purging the impurities and we, animals and humans, are asked to doing the same. We are being asked to treat each other with respect; to stop the senseless killing and panic peddling. Focus on what is most important for the collective whole.

You may have noticed that your body can't handle the chemicals it once could, or the stress it once tolerated. We are shifting, transforming our beings on all levels in order to move into the future. Struggling or fighting the evolution will only create more stress. To alleviate the distress you may be experiencing at this moment—before you move ahead into the text— I have included a creative visualization technique that I use frequently in order to keep myself in check. You can use this to center yourself when you feel as if your life is out of sorts.

> First, imagine or visualize a river. Consciously, you know that the river flows in one direction and as you see yourself stepping into the water, feel the weight of it push against your legs, allow yourself to give in to the force of the river. Imagine that you lie back, letting your arms and legs lift and float freely, playing atop the waters natural flow. Now, imagine that there is no longer any struggle left within you. You have given yourself to the river and *it* will take you to the place you are meant to be.

The purpose of this visualization is to help you with releasing the feeling that you have to fight or struggling in order to find your direction in life or change something that is going on around you now. If you see yourself entering the current, moving up stream, this is a clue that you are struggling with life, and quite possibly, unhappy with your successes. This also applies to those that see themselves enter the river, fighting the current to get to the other side. Here is an affirmation I use when I feel that I am trying too hard.

> Water spirit, I affirm that I will enter the depths
> of your soul, lift my feet and go with your flow.
> I trust you to take me where I need to be at this
> time in my life. This I affirm.

Great Spirit knows what your true path is, but we humans have a tendency to think that we have to get into the river and start paddling; fighting against the current in order to go where we *think* we need to be. We are our own worst enemy; creating most of the stresses in our lives.

I have to admit, there is one thing that I encounter while working with most clients that, even after twenty-five years, still perplexes me. It is the way we all seek to *belong* somewhere or to something like finding an organization or group of like-minded individuals that may or may not help us to define who we are. Each one has its benefits but each distances us from one another. Let us think on religion first. The Methodists, Catholics, and Jehovah's Witness, and so on, are merely examples of groups that believe in *something*. God, Jesus Christ, or something other than these; with each having its own twists and turns, and each person choosing that religion which, more often than not, chooses to sit in judgment over or criticize the others. I have to ask, *why?* Do you think our loving, compassionate God is judgmental or critical of us? I don't. We as humans tend to rip ourselves, as well as others, to shreds. Why would God waste time doing such a thing? The answer is-God wouldn't. We, who seek power and knowledge, do. We tend to look down on others in order to make ourselves feel better about our station in life.

I am hopeful that these writings will help you to see that we no longer have to struggle. We no longer have to look down upon others. In this *sacred time*, we can now raise ourselves to a place where we stand together; doing what is right by all and for all.

Our Native American ancestors believe that we are all made from the same matter, energy, and atoms. Being that we are all comprised of the same stuff means we are *all* connected and a part of everything that exists. Only we choose to separate ourselves in order to show our individuality; striving toward wealth or success, good health, happiness and peace only to find ourselves empty and in a state of aloneness. We have fallen short of our own expectations; not God's expectations of us because God does not possess the same mental state we do. We choose the good, bad, the different, or the indifferent. What God wants for us is universal peace inside and out. Being in touch with this truth gave me a thirst for knowledge, and this thirst led me to do more research into religious scholars and philosophers of days gone by.

Philosophy and Religion

A S WE MOVE through this chapter I would like to suggest that the weight of your attention be placed more on the thoughts and ideas of the philosophers and religious scholars and take with you the notion that each individual brought valuable information forth during their lifetime which may have directly or indirectly influenced how we each experience our world. What may not be as important is their life history, although I have added certain information so as to link each to their particular time periods, environments and outside influences; as I believe that we are each affected deeply by our interactions within our environments and relationships, and we each have something to offer up to others based on our own experiences within those milieus.

Let us begin with Ibn Rushd (1126–1198), who was an Islamic religious philosopher born into a notable Spanish-Arab family of jurists in Cordoba or Spain—

as we know it today. He lived at a distinct period in history when the disintegration of the Caliphate of Cordoba had led to the fragmentation of Muslim Spain among the muluk al-tawaif or Party Kings, that had been defeated by a band of fervent warriors and yielded to the epicurean atmosphere of Spanish Islam.

He trained in medicine and was accomplished in philosophy, religion, and theology. In his early years he became chief judge of Cordoba under the Almoravids, which had been a position his grandfather had once held before his death— during the year Rushd was born.

He was influenced by famous philosophers of generations past. Two such truth-seekers were thinker and writer Ibn Bajja of Saragossa, and his celebrated teachers Abu Jafar Harun al-Tajali of Trujillo. Both applied energy to expanding the rationalism of the Greek philosophical tradition into a powerful intellectual tool for seeking out truths concerning God, human beings and the world. Ibn Rushd/Averroes and Islamic Rationalism—the belief that thought and action should be governed by reason are confirmed in his works, *Long Commentary on the Metaphysics* (c.1290) which suggests that *the highest worship of God is to be found first and foremost in the philosophical science of metaphysics rather than in the rituals of religion.* (Ibn Rushd/Averroes and *Islamic* Rationalism)

Rushd became famous for his commentaries, which were his life's work, revolving around the writings of Aristotle. His quest for facts related to God and our human existence allowed him to differentiate between religion and philosophy. He believed that only metaphysicians were capable and proficient in interpreting doctrines contained in the prophetically revealed law and furthermore alleged that the aim of philosophy was to establish the true inner meaning of religious beliefs and convictions. (*Ibn Rushd-Averroes*) He believed that the world was not created but that it was eternal, and in order to prove his theory he used Aristotle's argument of *First Reason*, "There always was motion and always will be motion throughout all time, and we have explained what is the first principle of this eternal motion; we have explained further which is the primary motion and which is the only motion that can be eternal, and we have pronounced the first movement to be unmoved" (Aristotle, Physics, Book VIII, chapter 9) He moves on to prove this truth by using an interpretation of the Quran thereby expressing his opinion by stating urgings which support the opposite view of the arguments of his religious scholars, al-Ghazali and al-Ash'ari. (Al-Farabi and Ibn Rushd on the Correlation between Philosophy and Religion) Rushd was determined to draw the attention of representatives of religious teaching to philosophy and seek understanding, within their good company, of the world which surrounds human kind.

There is only one truth which is that religion is for everyone, no matter what religion that may be. That the whole and only truth for all believers is that religious teachings about reward, and punishment, and the hereafter must be accepted by the elite as well as by the masses. The philosopher must choose the best religion which for a Muslim is Islam—as preached by Muhammad, the last of the prophets—just as Christianity was the best religion at the time of Jesus and Judaism at the time of Moses. (Ibn Rushd/Averroes)

With the scope of this notion, it is my belief that although there are many religions, they all equal a one true philosophy. Furthermore, he believed that Islamic law conformed to the truth and conveys knowledge which supports happiness as the whole of creation, which is guaranteed. He trusted that everyone was permitted to their own share of happiness in this life as well in the next and that those who do not truly know God would be a believer merely through symbols rather than by evidence. He admits that Islamic law contains knowledge that exceeds our mortal perceptions however the divinely revealed truths should be accepted by everyone. He advocates that creation is a continuing process, which Aristotle demonstrated in the perpetuity of matter. He also asserts that God knows of details but that his wisdom is different from that of humans.

So why did I regurgitate this information into this text? Religion and philosophy are two forms of knowledge, which complete rather than nullify each other. (Al-Farabi and Ibn Rushd on the Correlation between Philosophy and Religion (247) Let us consider that philosophy is merely a tool used for understanding why we are here today and that religion could be used to better articulate and recognize our beingness. The Bible, religious, and philosophical teachings allow us to peek into the past; to see what others have learned and how to live a better life; possibly a life of oneness and faithfulness. Should we merely choose a religion based on symbols rather than having felt something stir within us providing the connection, we might be left feeling empty and disconnected in our religious principles.

I once had a friend that would ask me each Christmas eve whether I was going to go to church that evening. I found it quite interesting that he went no other time during the year except that night; seeking to be freed from any guilt of his wrong doings during that year. At the time I answered that I had not gone throughout the year but that had always been connected and in communication with God. I did not feel the need to go into a church to gain Gods acceptance or absolution.

Just as Rushd felt that religion and philosophy could understand one another; this would be appropriate for achieving the common purpose of reaching the truth, which also resonates with my own beliefs. He tried to harmonize the relationship between religion and philosophy; striving to draw the attention of representatives of religious teaching to philosophy and aimed to understand the world which surrounded humanity. We each are entitled to our own righteous practices as they relate to us. If by chance our practices are hurtful to others, then and only then would I say that we are not acting in the best interest of humanity and that we are out of balance with our sacred life.

Now let's take a lighthearted look at our religious and government systems. I choose to not spend much time on this topic, as my only intention for bringing this to light is to gain a better understanding of what is within our power to change.

Martin Luther, a monk plagued by disproportion between his own sense of sinfulness and the perfect righteousness God required for salvation. Money and power seemed to be the object of political and religious affection. Man presumed themselves to be above God; manipulating, controlling, and commanding; stepping on the meek and downtrodden to fulfill their lustful ideals, as they have since time began. What makes this time any different from years past? Choice and faith perhaps. We all know that someone has to take the first step in order for all others to follow. Rushd was moved by his search for truth; just as Aristotle, Hippocrates, Luther and others did.

During the late–Middle Ages, popular resentment of clerical immunities and ecclesiastical abuses spread among German cities and towns which yielded an unorganized *national* opposition to Rome's reform. Protest of indulgences and the theology that legitimated them.

Luther believed that the righteousness that God demands did not result from charitable acts and religious ceremonies, but was given full measure to anyone, and all, who believed in and trusted Jesus Christ as their perfect righteousness satisfying to God. He believed that faith without charitable service to one's neighbor was dead, not whether good works should be done, but how those works should be respected. He argued that it was unbiblical to treat works as contributing to one's eternal salvation and that this was only something that God could bestow. Good works expected over a lifetime, not because they earned salvation. The believer bound to Christ by faith already possessed Gods perfect righteousness. (pp. 274–275)

This is some pretty deep stuff, but my point is that, even today, we have a tendency to think along these lines. There are many that think that by doing for others we might be spared any suffering in Hell or Purgatory by God or some other personal religious entity of our choosing.

In Luther's day, indulgences paid would release the living of the obligation to perform a *work of satisfaction* for a sin, which Luther reacted to with anger and frustration; protesting the sale of indulgences that were being used to raise money for a new Saint Peters basilica in Rome. What he saw then was what he considered to be a circus, where people paid to be falsely discharged of their sins and freed of purgatory in the name of God. What makes now any different from Luther's experiences of the 1500s?

I do not believe that our salvation can be bought or sold but is something only we have the power to enforce within our own lives.

I, like you, have had my struggles as you are about to see and share. I may have been born with the exceptional gift of empathy and yet am still very much human and prone to error. In the pages to follow I choose to share what I have learned, and live to engage in faithful awareness; eager to live this life for as long as I am allowed to do so.

As the earth shifts and changes beneath us, this sacred time calls to us all. Something or someone is asking us to shift and change also. There is a divine intelligence at work here and many are feeling something tugging within them while others may only be experiencing the earth changes by seeing what is happening around them. Some may only be experiencing minor discomfort while others are driven to the emergency room to have major body work done. In this sacred time I suggest you pay attention. Your body may ache, your heart may be beating strangely, you have begun to feel and experience things differently than you once had. Note that something is waiting patiently as we align ourselves with the one divine truth. The truth that is ready to reveal a time where everything you say and do affects the tides, the weather, or it affects how other people view us, view themselves, how they treat each other, how they treat the animals, this planet, how they will affect future generations or even how it may affect extraterrestrial life forms. It's a time for integrity, honesty, true inner strength, humility, compassion and spiritual passion. It is time to clean ourselves up; to stop the killing, the thieving, and the raping of the people and the planet. It is time to find solutions to problems without depleting our natural resources, overpopulation, and deforestation. This is your sacred time and by writing this book it is my intention to provoke thought and sacred action. What will you do with it? Use this text to peer deeply into your future. What will you look like as you live your sacred life? To delete any old outmoded ideas about fear and lack, I suggest that you grasp the notion that this is the life that only you yourself can live, and that no one in the world has to do without in order for you to have it. You were born into this life with a particular skillset and only you are able to do the thing God sent you here to do.

As you move through each chapter you will get a sense of who I have become based on my own personal life experiences. The life I will be sharing with you is very real, it is mine and I cannot imagine being anything other than what and who I am. I am deeply moved and in love with the idea of a God source and it is within these pages that I pray you too get to know, understand and fall in love with it also.

Guide My Sheep

MY DEAR FRIEND, Mark Argo, had been sick, fighting cancer for quite some time. Nearing the end of his time in his physical body, I visited him on occasion to gently rub his hands and feet, to help him relax, and release some of the tension his body was experiencing and I was directed to spend time with him to help him fully understand and truly know compassion before he left this plane of consciousness.

The Saturday before he passed away, God told me I had to speak to him about leaving his physical body. As usual, I did not question what was being asked of me. I just did what I was told. Mark was in a hospital bed that Hospice had brought to his parents home to make him more comfortable. I entered the room, sat down beside him and began my usual reflexology routine on his hands. I sensed that he was very weak, and as I gazed into his eyes he was barely able to hold them open. I spoke to him softly and told him it was time for us to have a serious talk about letting go of his physical body. At the time I remember thinking to myself about having soul knowledge of a commitment I had made to my divine creator around broaching difficult discussions like this one. It was not an easy subject to talk about with Mark, but I was committed to that promise that was ingrained within me.

As I began speaking, his eyes opened wide as if to show me that he was in protest of this subject. Without hesitation he used energy he should have been saving and clearly stated that he did not want to talk about it right now. I gently spoke to his objection but said that Spirit was adamant about us having this conversation today—not later. I spoke to him about how powerful the human spirit is and how we could hear each other's thoughts merely by focusing our attention on it, but that we could also see things from within someone else if we placed our hands upon them, which is a technique that I had learned in my early twenties called psychometry. To show him how easy it was to read thoughts, I asked him to participate in an exercise with me. His wide eyes softened as I lightly touched his hand. As I allowed myself to open and connect to his energy, I could feel his weakness but I also felt the strength of his spirit.

I told him that I was thinking of a number between one and ten and I wanted him to tell me what the number was. In less than a second, he proclaimed that I was thinking of the number four. He was right. I was so excited; I practically jumped up on the bed with him. His poor emaciated body jumped as I expressed my enthusiasm. I felt awful for scaring him, but I couldn't contain my enthusiasm.

I knew he was exhausted so I moved on to prepare him for what was to come; being sure to respectfully express my compassion about his situation. Before I left him, I asked him if he would take a message to Great Spirit. The message went as follows: "Tell Jesus and God that I don't like this cancer thing and I think he should do something about it; people controlling cures are just not humane." Then finally as I pressed my forehead to his hands, I asked him if he would ask God a question for me. He nodded that he would.

"What am I supposed to be doing here?"

I ended our talk by telling him that once out of his physical body, he would find it easier to communicate with me. I told him I loved him and said goodbye. As I left, I knew it would be the last time I would see him in pain.

Mark Argo passed away the next Saturday. As he left his physical body his energy connected with mine and as he did, he said he had a message for me in answer to my statement and question. He said, "The cancer thing was not of God. He did not create cancer. That this was man's doing. Now, in answer to your question about what you are to do while here God said, 'Guide my sheep.'"

My life would be nothing without the love, wisdom, and guidance from God—our Great Spirit. I am truly grateful for the angelic assistance I received in facing and conquering my fears about sharing my life with you. As I meditated on how to begin, this inspired me to immerse myself in the river.

Message from God

AS I VISUALIZED myself entering the eternal waters I asked God if he had one message to share with the human race, what would that one message be. His reply opened my eyes.

> Congratulations. War is no longer a challenge. Men have perfected war. There is no integrity in war. Now rise to the challenge of perfecting peace. There is integrity.

> —GOD

Destiny

At the time, I had started writing this book I was thirty-eight years old. I had spent quite a bit of energy trying to figure out why I was put here up until the time Mark passed away. Great Spirit's answer gave me a foundation to stand on. Up to that point, I had just meandered through my life, helping where I felt I was called to, creating businesses, educating people on personal health issues, and trying to maintain my own sense of peace.

I worked hard no matter what I engaged in and I was aligned with good people that believed in and supported me in my endeavors. Nothing ever really came easy except for my ability to feel what others were feeling. When I use the term *easy* I mean to say that it was a gift or ability that came naturally to me. Of course I had to develop my ability further, with the help of different teachers over the course of twenty plus years, but what I experienced when *feeling* the energy of others, there came with it a sense of knowingness that I could not and would not dispute. Some mentors had come into my life and stayed while others went on to work with other very gifted individuals. They are all very special spiritual beings, and I am truly grateful for their compassionate guidance and wisdom.

When Great Spirit said that I was to guide his sheep, I felt a bit uneasy because I had no plan; no clue about what to do, where to go, or who to help. So I called out to Great Spirit and shared my hesitation with beginning my work. I asked Spirit to send me someone that could help me further define my life work to fulfill the job of guiding his followers. It wasn't long after I had asked that I was sent a guide. What was interesting is that this person was someone I was already acquainted with. He was already a client/student of mine, but this time he would take the posture of teacher. Teacher-student, student or teacher, it does not matter which one we are today. The only thing that matters is that we show up and do what is asked of us—be it to learn or to teach.

I believe it was during the year of 2003 when Gregg Spieth took the posture of teacher to me, and he has remained faithfully compassionate, trusting in God's processes and open to this day. When I shared the Mark Argo story with Gregg he lit up with enthusiasm and told me that he knew what I needed to do to further define my path in life. He shared his story about how he found something that was helping him. The book he shared was written by Lance Secretan and its title is *Inspirational Leadership: Destiny, Calling and Cause*. I will refer to specific questions taken from Secretan's book in order to show you how I found more direction. In requesting permission to share his information with you, his Executive Assistant confirmed that I was allowed to do so by reminding you these works came from an earlier version. Secretan's new updated version *The Spark, the Flame and the Torch* can be found by visiting his website http://www.secretan.com/books-dvds/the-spark-the-flame-the-torch

I used Secretan's questions in order to connect to my higher purpose and lead me to my destiny. The workbook came with instructions on how to use the worksheets which made my quest that much easier. When I first began reading through his questions I felt as if I would never be able to put anything on the paper. I overthought the process and tried to make sense of it right from the start which is something he suggests you not do. He does not want you to worry about making your answers pretty or perfect; he just wants you to write. You are then supposed to sit and meditate on your answers; reviewing what you had written in order to see what themes surface.

"As *destiny* has to do with your personal purpose, what you are passionate about and how you see yourself contributing to making the world a better place; *cause*, is connected to the here-and-now and should lead to your destiny; and *calling*, is the work we love and how we are when we are *in the flow*." (Lance Secretan)

I committed myself to this process because I knew I wanted to make a difference while here in this body. I began asking myself questions like, "How hard can it be to find my true calling?

"How hard are you going to make it," I heard my inner voice reply.

Have others been successful with this process? I thought to myself. Then I realized I was already making it hard. I was over analyzing the process instead of diving in and doing it. More thoughts flooded my brain, "*Okay dummy, let go!*"

My questions and answers proceeded as follows:

- What is the uniqueness within you that calls to be lived?

  My answer: As I dug in I meditated on the question. The answer came through as follows; Deep Faith—a knowing—my ability to feel what others feel; to be a voice for those that don't have one, or do not know how to share what they feel; the ability to guide others to a space of understanding themselves physically mentally, emotionally, and spiritually;

to awaken the *spirit* in everyone that seeks to truly know.

- Is there community, national, or world issues that you feel passionately about changing?

  My answer: Disappointment, anger, murder, stress, lack of integrity, lack of honesty, resentment, greed, jealousy, lack of passion, and fear based thinking.

- How will you inspire divine results?

  My answer: Guide others that are ready to make a change. Teach by example. By sharing my personal quest for peace and prosperity– Walk it – don't just talk it!

- How does your time here and the role you have assumed create enhancements and bliss in your life and in the lives of everyone with whom you are connected with?

  My answer: Being at one with what I feel or knowing that I may not want to be at one with what I feel coming from others. Just by choosing one or the other, to feel or not to feel, and knowing that I am who I am which, enhances every day of my life.

- What are your divine gifts to be shared?

  My answer: Empathy, passion, compassion, faith, vision, a deeper level of perception, and intuition.

As you can see, all of my answers were a bit fragmented. I just wrote what came to mind and did not try to rip the information to shreds as it came through. I just let it be.

The exercise worked like a charm. It really helped me see the reoccurring themes in my life. It was much easier to move forward once I realized that I was here to serve and guide others to find clarity in their lives. I sat and reflected on my answers from the destiny, calling and cause process and began to ask my spirit more questions.

"How can I begin to do what I have come here to do?"

Spirit answered, "Release."

"I feel as though something hinders my progress. What is it?"

Spirit answered, "Memories."

"So what do I need to do to get past the memories?"

Spirit answered, "You need to visit the memories stored in every cell in your body in order to move forward."

"But, I don't think the past has anything to do with who I am right now. The past is the past. Why go back to rehash these things when it is all done and over with?"

Spirit answered, "Everything you have experienced in your life is stored within every cell of your body. Good, bad, or otherwise. In order to be at one with yourself you must visit these memories and view them to see the patterns or habits that you have carried. Feel them and allow your body to cry, laugh, and detoxify them one by one."

"So you are saying that everything I have ever experienced is stored in my body as cellular memory?"

Spirit answered, "Yes."

"And you say that in order for me to see my habits and patterns, I must revisit these memories?"

Spirit answered, "Yes."

"All of them?"

Spirit answered, "As many as your body needs you to see and feel in order to create a release; if that means you view all of them in order to create a healing on the cellular level, then yes, all of them."

"How do I begin?"

Spirit answered, "Focus your attention on any aches and pains your body is bringing to your attention. One by one, ask each pain what emotion lies within it. You may need to use some deep breathing exercises to help bridge the body and mind. Breathe in through your nose until your lungs are completely full. Hold three seconds. Breathe out of your mouth until your lungs are totally empty; releasing all stale air at the bottom of your lungs. Repeat the process three times, or until you begin to feel dizzy. Once you experience this dizziness you can return to your normal breathing. This breathing exercise is extremely helpful in stopping the internal chatter in your head so you are more apt to hear what your body is trying to tell you. Try this and then we will move on."

I surveyed my body. Okay, my tongue hurts a bit today. I asked what emotion is stored within. It seemed as if my tongue began to tremble and it took a minute or two for the answer to come. When it did, the word terror appeared boldly typewritten in my minds eye. "So now, Spirit, I know that terror resides in my tongue... what's next?"

Spirit answered, "Ask the tongue to show you to the very first memory the body has stored within it around that particular emotion. I asked my tongue to show me and *wham*— there it was.

I was standing on the bank of the Delaware River watching my father and my brother race boats. My brother's engine had shut down. He couldn't get it started so he shimmied to the front end of the boat and began to paddle with his hands to draw the boat to the shoreline. I am not sure but I look to be about five years old. I remember being so worried about his safety because the other boats were continuing to race and he could have gotten hit by one of them.

What was truly amazing about this method of exploration was that as soon as I saw the memory attached to the emotion, my tongue stopped hurting.

Detoxifying Memories

F ROM 2004 THROUGH 2005, I became very good at finding the memories stored in my body and listening to my organs. I thought I knew my body before I started using this technique but quickly came to realize just how detached I had been throughout my adolescence and into mid-twenties.

In May of 2004, my husband and I were teaching a Be A Responsible Server's (BARS) class at Lowes Motor Speedway in Concord North Carolina. I had been having panic attacks on occasion since 9-11, and I was really getting tired of them running my life, so I initiated a conversation with Great Spirit about how fed up I was. I wanted to know why my body was having such a hard time. Now, I was plagued by strange feelings nagging at me like a rabid dog biting at my ankles. I use to love drinking wine but found out that my body didn't like it any longer. Each time I tried to take a sip, my throat would close up, I couldn't swallow and the panic attacks commenced. During this month in 2004, Great Spirit came to me and told me that I could not continue on this path. Spirit said that my life was to change dramatically, and the only way I was going to survive this change was to purge my perceptions associated with the memories that were stored within my cells. Spirit said that I could no longer be who I thought myself to be and that I must change without rebellion.

As I look back on this, I realize that I was not afraid on a soul level. Of course, my body quaked as Spirit shared what was to be undertaken, but I remember feeling as if I was ready to accept my task whole heartedly and open myself to the process.

Back to the speedway story! On this particular day, my husband Monty and I were to be at Charlotte Motor Speedway acting as Alcohol Monitors. We, and our off duty police officers, would walk the speedway in search of underage consumers to keep our servers from getting into trouble with alcohol beverage control. Monty and I were getting ready to head out when he stopped me and asked me to sit down. He relayed to me that over the past few days he noticed me getting edgy and short with people. Of course I noticed also but I told him I couldn't possibly sit at home feeling agitated; I had to go to work and feel like I was doing something productive. He tried to make light of the fact that my edginess would not be tolerated out at the race track and that he would not be able to protect the drunks from me, so I was not allowed to go with him. I pitched a pretty big fit but my outburst fell on deaf ears as he left me to ponder my anxiety and protest.

I paced the floors for a bit; let the dogs in and out and finally sat down to rest on the couch. I switched on the TV and found myself watching a movie with Bruce Willis and Demi Moore in it, which was quite negative. Blood, anger, lots of yelling. I felt like I had fallen into a very bad dream. When I realized that my brain couldn't handle another minute of the movie, I changed the channel and went back to slouching on the couch. Again, I found myself watching another negative movie. I felt strange all over. I had never felt like this before. It was like there was two of me crammed into this one body.

Then it started. I heard a voice say "Go get a drink."

I looked at the clock on the TV, it was five pm. I thought, *What in God's name was that?*

I turned down the TV volume. It came again. "Go get yourself a drink."

I thought for a moment and answered. "No, I don't want a drink.

The voice answered me back, "Yes you do."

"No I don't," I thought back.

"Yes you do," it boomed back at me. "You will feel better if you do."

I was beginning to get upset, and then it hit me. Great Spirit told me that I was going to have to purge and change. It felt as if bombs were going off inside of my body. I started pacing the floors and I was not feeling very well. I remembered the process of revealing cellular memories and decided it was time to begin the process. I took a deep breath and went back to my battle with the voice.

I began by asking the voice why it felt as though alcohol would make me feel better. It was quick to reply.

"In the past when you have been upset and drank, and you felt better." The voice boomed as if challenging me. "The alcohol will not judge you, it will not criticize you. It is your friend!"

Instead of fighting with the voice, I asked more questions. "Why do you want a drink, I asked?"

"You're lonely," it said.

"No I'm not," I said.

"Yes you are!"

"No I'm not."

"Yes you are!"

This could have gone on all day long if I let it, so I quickly moved to the next question.

"Alright, if it is as you say and I'm lonely, what memory is attached to this loneliness?" *Boom!* There it was. Bells, whistles, and bombs were going off inside of me as the memory came flooding forward. Archetypical tornados ripped through trees and houses in my mind's eye. There I was, in my bed above my health store in New Jersey—as if living the memory all over again.

It was five in the morning and the phone was ringing. I woke myself just enough to answer it. My father was on the other end of the line. I leaned over to look at the time and then realized something was wrong—he never called me. He hesitated as he told me that there had been an accident.

"Nicole, its your father. Wake up. I need to know you are awake."

"Okay Dad, I am up. What's is it?" I said.

"Your brother had an accident" Maybe I was still asleep but, time seemed to stand still.

"What? No. What? Do you need me to get on a plane and head to North Carolina?"

"No."

He kept dancing around something and I had to almost pry it out of him. I kept asking questions until-finally, after much goading, he told me that Craig had died on the scene and I could not fix it.

I don't know where the horrific sound came from. I slid off my bed and onto the floor with arms out-stretched in front of me on the carpet and howled like a wolf caught in a trap. "Noooooooooo!"

Minutes passed but seemed like hours had been wasted. I don't even know if I took a breath until I real-ized that my father was still on the phone. I gathered myself and took a deep breath.

"Dad, I am sorry. I can only imagine how you are feeling right now. Are you okay and can I do anything to help you?"

"Yes, I need you to go tell your mother."

"No way in hell Dad. No way am I going to tell my mother that her baby is dead. NO way!"

I heard him stammer. "O-Okay", he said.

I took another deep breath and chose my words carefully. "However, I will go over there and be there when you call her so that she is not alone."

"Okay. Your older brother is on his way down with Maggie and the girls. He should be there soon. I will give you both some time to get there."

We hung up and I dressed as quickly as I could. Fortunately mom and I lived one house away from each other. I lived at 1 South Railroad Avenue-above the store, my friend Harriet lived next to me at 3 South Railroad and mom was at 5 South Railroad Avenue in Stockton New Jersey.

I stepped out into the early morning darkness, leaving the warmth of the house behind me. I took note of the stillness in the air. It was so quiet, it was almost unnerving. I passed Harriets house. Her livingroom light was on, but it was too early for her to be awake. As I stepped onto my mother's front porch I paused and took a long deep breath. I wondered what I would say when she awoke to find me in her livingroom at 5:30 in the morning for no good reason. I looked into the sky and then turned to open the door. Mom was lying asleep on the couch. This was normal, or at least it had been her normal since she first saw a dark figure in her bedroom—a ghost she said—and one night after a number of sightings it tried to strangle her while she lay sleeping. That was it for her. She would not sleep up there again. Amazingly she lived in that house for a number of years but avoided sleeping upstairs.

She awoke. "Nik, what are you doing here so early?"

"I thought I would come have a cup of tea with you before I go to work", I heard myself say. Not at all sure of who said it. While I fumbled with my thoughts all I could think about was whether she would ever forgive me for lying to her.

She got up and walked off toward the bathroom while I helped myself to the tea pot; filling it with water.

"Nik, its too early for you to be up. What's going on?"

I couldn't sleep mom. I turned the stove on and headed back to the front door to see if my brother had shown up to save me. I peered out the glass door and as mom came back to the livingroom behind me I dodged her questions by stepping out on the front porch. *Darn!* I thought. I am screwed. She is going to hate me for this. I stepped out to the porch steps and looked into the imposing star filled sky. I could hear mom calling me from the couch. I ignored her, praying Dean would come around the corner.

I began to cry, and in the release I cursed God for taking away my laughter and putting us in this position. "God, how dare you take him from us. After all I do for you—helping your children without ever asking for anything in return. I will never do another days work for you-not ever again!"

To my surprise a deep masculine voice boomed back at me from the still dark morning sky. "Don't be so hasty. We understand your feelings, but hear us,…we will allow you the time you need to heal, however you cannot separate yourself from us. You are one of us."

"Not anymore", I snapped. "I am done!" Just as I made my declaration I saw Dean and Maggie's car lights coming around the corner. I took a deep breath and headed back into the house.

Mom saw Dean's vehicle pull up out front. Now she realized something was up. She stood up and looked at me perplexed. "Nik, what's going on?" She faultered and was now holding her chest.

Dean entered just in time. "Mom, the phone is going to ring in a minute and you need to answer it," I said. The phone rang. "Mom...Dad is calling, please answer the phone", I said.

Mom began to cry. Dean stood facing her and I stood to her back, both of us essentially sandwiching her in-holding her up as Dean handed her the phone.

The minutes that followed were blurred and distorted. While mom spoke to dad, I sent my energy to North Carolina to find Craig as I did for many days after in an effort to communicate with him to be sure his spirit would be alright. From what I was told he had passed around 11:30 p.m. so I figured that his spirit would be locked into a cycle, not knowing that he had passed. As I watched my energy move over the encompassing area and onto Dads property I found Craig. His spirit ran from the accident scene up the road, down Dad's driveway to the house, into the house and up the stairs, calling for our father. I followed him and entered the house between the two floors on the staircase.

"Dad...Dad! Dad where are you? Something happened and I need to talk to you", he said.

I watched, trying to figure out how I could get him to stop running and see me. I watched him anxiously as he ran past me on the stairwell each time the scene replayed itself. It was like being in a horror film. He could not see me or hear me. Then, after the third time watching this distressing event, I remembered what my mentor had told me years before. She had said that I would have to project my energy into the heart of the house and anchor myself there in order to connect to that spirit. As he ran past me I anchored myself into the staircase and hallway like a tree anchoring its roots into the ground and spoke to him from my solar plexus.

"Craig, stop!"

As he passed me this time he felt my energy. "Nik? He spun around to face me. "What are you doing here? I thought you were in New Jersey."

"I am Craig."

"Nik-where is Dad? There was an accident and I need to find him."

"Craig, Dad is in Atlanta Georgia—Remember?—It's the weekend of the last NASCAR race of the season."

"Oh yeah! I almost forgot-I am supposed to head down there-Dad's waiting for me. He shook that off as if trying to shift his thinking. "Well, there was this wreck down the road just past Dale Earnhardts place. The guy in the accident died!"

"I know Craig. That guy in the accident…that guy was you."

His spirit stood before mine in that lonely hallway staircase and he did not waiver. I felt his anger rise. I motioned to try to touch him but he pushed me away and retreated through the stairwell door.

After Dad spoke with Mom to tell her what the parametics had told him about the accident the three of us sat in silence, caught in our own dark thoughts. Mine went back to my conversation with Craig in

North Carolina. What would happen next? Where did Craig's spirit go when he left me in the stairwell at Dad's? Then my thoughts quickly jumped back to Dad. He said he would fly in and the funeral would be held there in New Jersey, but he also wanted to have a memorial service in North Carolina for some of Craig's friends. After Mom settled down Dean and I headed back to our respective homes to shower and get dressed for company. As I meandered back to my place I called on a couple of spirit friends that I had assisted in times past. I asked them to find Craig and tell him all they could about where he was and what would happen next. They were happy to assist and I was glad to have a bit of time to collect my thoughts before the family started showing up.

I had just enough time to shower and dress when I heard my store door creak at the bottom of health-store stairwell. The door did not physically open, but it sounded as if it had. I was quite familiar with this noise being that the store and house seemed to act as a train station for every spirit coming or going through Stockton New Jersey. At times I found it difficult to sleep due to some nasty wayward spirit banging on my basement door at all hours of the night.

I walked to the top of my stairs to catch a glimpse of my visitors. There they were-the two spirits I had called on an hour earlier. I motioned to them to suggest that I was upstairs. "So…where is he?" I said.

"He is at the morgue trying to get back into his body," they said in unison. "You need to come help, he is very upset."

I sat down on my bed and closed my eyes, projecting my spirit to Mooresville North Carolina not far from my father's house. I followed the two spirits through a door that led into the morgue to see my brother trying to merge with the shell of a body that lay unmoving upon the table.

"Craig! What are you doing?"

"I am not dead. I want back in! This has to work— *damn it*—he growled, shooting me a penetrating glance that left goosebumps on my skin. "*Help me!*" he groaned. "Help! I do not want to be dead." Just then his spirit sat, half lifted from the body lying on the table. "Nik, something tastes funny."

"Craig, I am sorry, I cannot change this. Your body has been gone for too long. You had the accident around 11:30 p.m. and it is now 12 hours later. Your body can no longer sustain your spirit. You are going to have to let go honey- I am so sorry."

He moved away from the table sobbing and went through the wall; perching himself dejected and forlorn on the curb outside. I allowed my spirit to follow. I told him that I had to go but that I had asked the two spirits to stay with him to help him. I would check back later to see how he was doing. I made a mental note of what I felt coming from his energy, as if I was inside of his body living the experience with him. Now, here I am 10 years after his death, reliving the entire incident all over again.

I thought it was painful the first time but here it was happening all over again. My worst nightmare was repeating itself. The only difference this time was that I was truly immersed in the experience and there was no way to mask the emotions that was stored within my body. For years I stayed focused on helping the family cope with his death but did not allow myself to express my anger and sadness. I managed to lose myself during the month that followed Craig's death. It was easy; all I had to do was help everyone else and forget about myself; only this time I could not disregard the loneliness that surfaced from deep within my core. The memory then changed. I saw myself walking from my health store around the block every night—just after five in the afternoon—to go to the liquor store to purchase a bottle of wine. I'd go back home and polish it off and fall into bed drunk, wake up at five a.m. to go to work, come home and do it all over again. I did this for an entire month starting November 9th and finally, came to rest on December 10th of 1994. All I could muster each day was to go to work and then get drunk. I woke on December 10th hearing the bold masculine voice of Great Spirit. "You know you are no good to anyone in this state. You are going to end up with your brother unless you change your ways."

So I did. I decided to stop drinking like that, but I didn't stop drinking. The habit or pattern had been anchored in on a cellular level, and every night at five o'clock I would have a drink. I could have a couple of drinks and stop, but the fact remained that at five every night, I had to have at least two drinks or I wouldn't feel good.

Augh! It was like being punched in the gut all over again. Sirens went off in my brain, and I jumped from my seat and ran to the bathroom. Tears flowed like a river and I sobbed like a child, choking on each breath

I took. I found myself staring into the mirror at my own tear drenched eyes—searching for answers—only finding pain and hurt. I decided I needed to speak to someone and not just anyone would do. I really didn't think that anyone would understand what I was putting myself through but I had to speak to somebody. I picked up the phone and dialed Monty's cell number. When he answered I could hear the roar of the NASCAR race cars and fans cheering them on in the background. Knowing he would be pressed for time, I tried to explain what had just happened to me. He tried desperately to calm me, but he was unsure of what he was supposed to be doing to help. He couldn't stay on the phone with me because he was in the middle of arresting someone for underage drinking. So he did what any husband might when put into a situation where he had no understanding; he asked me to go speak to his mother. I tried to explain to him how hard it was for me to share this side of me that I had this overwhelming urge to drink and that if I stayed in this house, I would end up doing just that. He reluctantly told me that he had to hang up, and as I began sobbing again, he told me I should go outside with the dogs and go next door to speak to his mother.

I gathered myself up, hollered to the dogs, and headed for the front yard. I got about twenty-five feet from the front door and started pacing back and forth in the yard. "Do I go to Ida's, or do I go back inside for a drink?" I realized that I had not asked enough questions to make an informed decision, so I knelt in the yard and called for the dogs to come comfort me. I dug deep. "Why was I having so much trouble with the idea of talking with someone about this?"

With no effort on my part, aside from asking the question, the internal voice answered just as it had before, "Because they will criticize you."

"So I am afraid that people will criticize and judge me?"

"Yes!" The voice boomed back. "The alcohol is your friend, it doesn't make you feel bad, it doesn't tell you what to do, and it just lets you be you!"

This was amazing to me. I had no idea that all these years I had allowed this to manifest and smolder inside of me. My cells were carrying memories, painful memories that were delegating authority over my life in negative ways. I realized that I had to break the cycle. Now was the time. I stood up, called the dogs to follow me, and headed up the hill to Ida's house. I forced myself to open up to her and explained what was happening to me; I told her that I needed someone to listen to my intellectual vomit and that Monty had suggested that I talk to her.

She was very receptive and explained that she had gone through some very hard times with her husband over the use of alcohol, and that she had all the time in the world to listen to me.

As it turned out I had never spoken so much, or for so long, at one time in my whole life. I had rambled on about things that I had long forgotten, thought funny, or just plain stupid. We laughed; I cried and yammered on until after midnight. I could not believe the memories stored within me. Ida was a true angel that night and if she hadn't been there for me, I am sure I would not have fared so well. I spent the next two weeks purging memories and talking into the wee hours of each night. Monty shaking his head in disbelief that someone would put themselves through such nonsense was beyond his comprehension. He saw no reason for it. I tried to explain that Great Spirit had told me that in order for me to move forward in life I would have to purge. I was told that my new way of life could not possibly be sustained by such a damaged body. Our days and nights were spent in opposition to one another— a good portion of his energy was consumed by being furious with me for being so headstrong.

I remember we were up until four one morning, talking about the process I was committed to. I was trying to give him an example of Gods will over my own and explained this way.

"Okay Monty, if God came to you and said, 'I am here to take away your Parkinson's disease, will you let me heal you.' What would your decision be?"

He stood in the doorway starring out at the morning sky and to my surprise he actually answered me honestly. He said, "I don't know."

Wow! That took guts to admit, but I quickly jumped back to making my point and explained further. Although God was not healing me of Parkinson's disease or some equally disabling ailment, he was offering me a freedom; a chance to further define my life's work through him. In order to get a glimpse of this, I had to give up my antiquated ways of thinking and clean up all the cellular waste that lingered within me.

We ended our discussion, but I don't know whether he was just tired of talking or if he actually understood. I would prefer to think that by God's grace and glory he started to get it!

For two weeks, he watched me cry like never before. He did not try to interrupt the process. After the first two weeks, I felt clean for the first time in my life, but the memories still kept coming up; only now, they were hilarious to me, so much so that I spent the next two weeks in stitches laughing almost incessantly like a lunatic. Knee buckling, no breath, mouth wide open, laughing so hard I was crying kind of laughter. I had not laughed like that since I was a young child. You know the kind where you're laughing so hard you pee your pants?

As quickly as it had begun, it stopped. Only now I felt 10 pounds lighter. I slept like a rock which was not normal for me. There was no more internal chatter. No body aches to speak of, just total and complete balance.

Now I was ready-or so I thought!

Monty headed to bed around 10:30 this particular evening. I decided to stay up because I felt like I was waiting for something. I sat half watching the TV, but I had the sound turned down. I looked at the clock, which indicated that it was 11:10. I began to feel as though someone was pulling me from my body. I called out to Great Spirit and asked if I was okay. The reply was so startling that I slid from my chair and ended up on my knees.

"You will be just fine after your near death experience!" I heard the masculine voice say.

My body began to tremor, my sight dimmed, and my blood ran cold. I panicked. A few moments later, I pulled myself to my feet and made it into the bedroom where Monty lay sleeping. I crawled into bed beside him and curled up in the fetal position praying that if it was my time to go, I would be allowed to go peacefully and quietly so that I wouldn't wake Monty. Great Spirit assured me that it would not happen right then but that I was to do as I was told and everything would be all right.

I freaked! I was beside myself with fear as to how and when this near death experience would play out. I was not so bothered by the dying part but rather the "how". I just could not figure out why this was happening to me. Even without asking a direct question the answer came quickly.

"Nicole, we spent a month cleaning you up so that your body and spirit would make it through an experience of great importance. This is not something that you can shy away from. People will learn from this. People need to know about what you will have endured. You must proceed and have complete faith that I will be with you."

That summer passed with little issue. Then one cool day in November I heard the deep masculine voice of Great Spirit call me to action. Now, in order for you to understand, I will need to go back to 2003 when I had a surgery to have a hemorrhaging ovarian cyst removed due to endometriosis. I was still having minor abdominal pain, so I called my gynecologist to see if she would take a look at me. When I went in to see her, she suggested that I try a drug called luprelide acetate. She explained that it would push my body into a temporary state of menopause but that the side effects would be minor hot flashes, some mild headaches but nothing too extreme. My inclination was that this would not be a necessary move for me, but before I could decline the injection Great Spirit offered its two cents worth.

"Take the shot and I will be by your side, trust and have faith."

I heard myself agreeing to the shot even though my body dreaded doing it. The physician's assistant prepared the needle, gave it to me, and sent me on my way. It took all of five minutes to prepare and administer it, and the thought crossed my mind that I was being silly about such a small injection—there was nothing to it.

As I got in my vehicle, I asked Spirit why I was supposed to take the shot even though my body felt as if it was a bad move. Spirit said there are people that will need to hear your story. My sharing would save many lives. "Be brave, and I will be by your side," were the final words.

As I pulled out of the parking lot I thought to myself, *Oh my Lord, what had I gotten myself into?* All I could do now was trust that God would be with me and that I would make it through whatever was to come.

My Most Difficult Journey

I BELIEVE THAT THERE is a place for pharmaceutical drugs in the world; if not for any other
reason than to keep individuals alive that suffer
from illnesses that require this sort of intervention.
Despite my belief in their use many medications are
accompanied by undesirable secondary effects that can
shatter beliefs, cause other health ailments, and test the
strongest person. This story is a very personal one. It is
for no other reason than my trust and faith in God that
I am here today to share this with you.

Having been diagnosed with endometriosis my
physicians removed my left ovary, a hemorrhaging cyst
and part of my fallopian tube. A few weeks later my
physician suggested that I take a a specific medication
which was supposed to lessen the pain associated with
this disorder. Surprisingly, it only took two weeks for
the side effects from the drug to start. At first it was
just mild hot flashes and I remember thinking that if

these were the only side effects, I would be able to do this standing on my head.

In 1999 I became the proud owner of a patent on a race car simulator training system and its method, of which would allow race car drivers and teams to test, train and race within a virtual environment in order to save themselves travel time, money for travel related expenses and the potential of wrecking their cars or putting their lives at risk. To the best of my recollection, it was around 2003 or 2004 that I had determined that there were companies infringing. The founder of this one particular company agreed to meet with me in North Carolina to discuss this potential issue. When the first hot flash hit I was in this very meeting at the Chamber of Commerce sitting across from the company's owner, his engineer, my attorney and CPA.

Now, most women know what I mean when I say that it is difficult to let such a thing pass without notifying everyone else in the room. You feel like they can tell anyway by the look on your face so it is almost always necessary to explain that your body is about to spontaneously combust.

Just as the hotflash subsided, my thoughts fell to the side effects that I had read about in the medication disclaimer and I began to contemplate whether some other side effects would follow. I made it through the meeting and set for a day and time to negotiate but by that time my life was being ripped to shreds. I was right to have given thought to whether more side effects were to come as there certainly were more to follow. Within a few weeks of my meeting with the simulation company the blinding headaches started. Then the severe heart pulsations and chest pain came. One month into the drug interactions I was not able to eat because I had cysts growing in my throat and my throat was raw beyond anything you can imagine. Baby food became my mainstay. My brain felt as if it would explode through the back of my eyeballs. I could see no color. My world became black and white and with each passing day the white got darker and darker until I could no longer see to drive or work. I could not think straight enough to relay even a simple thought. No one understood what was happening to me. I kept trying to find a doctor to help me, but they were all saying that there was nothing wrong with me. I was living a total nightmare and to top it off, my husband thought I was losing my mind-and finally, so did I.

While he enjoyed his evenings watching TV or playing on the computer, I found it hard to venture out of the bedroom. I could not watch TV, listen to the radio, or play on the computer. I had unplugged every piece of electronic gadgetry I could get my hands on. Every time I tried to get near anything electronic my body became highly sensitive and I was thrown into anxiety-like attacks. I was ultra-sensitive to energy sources to begin with but now the medication just pushed me over the edge. Then, out of nowhere, the bad dreams started. I hadn't had nightmares since I was four years old. The first dream to get my attention rocked my world!

I was driving to Charlotte North Carolina in my 1997 Jeep Sahara. It appeared that I was dressed for a business meeting. The sun was shining and the day was cool but bright. Even though it was as dream I took note that everything was crisp, well-defined and very colorful. Without warning, as I was traveling in the southbound lane of highway 85, there was a large tanker truck painted to look like the fruity *lifesaver* wrapper. That struck me as odd. I felt as though my spirit was being pulled from my body and all of the sudden that tanker shot across the concrete center barrier breaking its rear axle, and the front wheels were heading for my jeep on the southbound side. You would be amazed at what comes to mind when you think you're going to die. I am not sure if it was miliseconds or seconds that had passed; but I found myself wondering whether slowing the vehicle would keep the truck from hitting me. What if I turned? Then, I quickly realized that either way I was going to die so I stopped fighting it. I called out in my mind to my parents. *Mom, Dad, I have to go, but I love you very much.* Then *Wham!* The tractor and its trailer landed smack dab on top of my jeep crushing my head.

I awoke with a jolt. I was afraid to open my eyes for fear of what I might see. I thought I was dead or worse, disfigured beyond recognition. I began breathing deeply just to be sure that my lungs were in working order. I chose not to feel around for my legs just in case one of both were missing. Then I slowly opened my eyes. The dream had been so devastatingly real. I thought for sure I would open my eyes to find doctors and nurses huddled around me hard at work. *Whew!* It was just a dream. My brain kicked into survival mode. What did this all mean? Was it a vision of something to come?

How could I possibly get behind the wheel of a vehicle after this experience? My evaluation of the dream went on for about a week and then the second dream came thundering in. I was again traveling southbound on 85 toward Charlotte. There was a tractor trailer; a flat-bed trailer, painted red, driving along in front of me. This was the second time I had seen vivid colors in my dreams. To my left was another big rig passing me. He appeared to be in a hurry. As he passed and got ahead of the flat bed driver something happened ahead that made me swerve into the right lane. This made the flat bed rig slam on his brakes and cut his wheels to the right very hard which put his trailer sideways in front of my jeep. I heard myself call out to my parents again in my mind, letting them know that I had to go. The jeep was being ripped apart by the flat bed and I found myself being thrown around outside of its shell. I could barely stand to keep my eyes open as I became a not so willing participant within the scene that played itself out. I saw myself heading straight for the tractor trailers rear tires. I was so close I could smell the rubber. The tires felt hot and sticky as my head was being crushed by their weight.

I awoke dazed and exhausted. This time I knew it was a dream, so I lay there breathing deeply mulling over all the symbols within the dream to determine what was most like the first one I had a week earlier. Keeping myself calm, I established that my head had been crushed. I thought of the headaches I had been having and, the feeling associated with my brain swelling made me think that this all must be related to the medication I had been given. How could one small shot have such intense side effects?

I quickly dismissed my mental investigation when I realized that something was standing next to the bed where my husband Monty lay sleeping. Now mind you, I have seen spirits and ghosts since I was about four years old; this was nothing like that. He-or IT-appeared to be in his mid-forties, about five foot nine inches tall. Since I was not seeing things in color, he appeared as a grayish mist-like figure. He leaned over Monty toward me and tried to hand me a knife. He said "Here, take this. You can stab him just like this,"—he mimicked the motions—and he'll never know the difference." My heart leapt. I couldn't breathe. I threw the covers back and jumped out of bed and ran from the bedroom. I tried to calm myself down and breathe. I felt as though I was under water, and I was afraid to take a breath for fear of drowning. I paced the living room floor. My heart was fumbling around in my chest. My breathing was irregular, and the pain in my chest was excruciating. I knew of nothing else to do but get on the treadmill and run. I would either run until I dropped dead or until that thing in the bedroom disappeared. I was not going to let that thing get me or make me hurt anyone-ever!

Now, I'm sure at this point you understand that there was no knife. I was hallucinating. The hallucinations went on for days. The next one came the very next morning. He—the shadow man—woke me up at six in the morning. This time he showed me cutting up my arms; shredding myself. Once again, I jumped out of bed and ran to the other room to get on the treadmill. Again, I ran until I felt like I was going to drop. My chest ached so badly. The pain was so bad it made me think and feel as if I was going to have a heart attack. As the hallucinations progressed I chose to keep them a secret. Each morning I'd repeat the process over and over again with the shadow man tormenting me like a spirit from purgatory luring me into his own excruciatingly brutal hell. The proverbial straw broke the camels back when the same shadow man woke me-just as he had been each morning. He took me by the hand and pulled me from the bed. He explained that my life was over. That I would never succeed at anything, ever! No one loved me and as a matter of fact, they have never cared for me, and I might as well just end my life. He walked me out the back door and through the yard toward the garage. As we approached the backside of the garage he pulled me close and forced a gun in to my hands. He said, "This is it! Pull the trigger; your life is over." He gripped the gun with my hand wrapped around it tightly; my finger under his as he pulled the trigger. My head exploded. I leapt straight out of bed and headed for the treadmill. I spent an hour racing as hard and fast as I could, trying with all I had within me to fight the feelings of defeat. When I finally stepped off the treadmill, I was drenched with sweat and tears.

Monty wasn't home, and I had no one to talk to. I felt like I couldn't call my mother or any of my friends for fear that they would not understand. I began to pray and asked God to help me through. Every thought and action from this point on was done slowly and with deliberate accuracy. I lit some candles and began to fill the bathtub. As I stripped out of my clothes, I tried to calm my mind. No matter how hard I had tried to remain peaceful, it tried harder to gain power over me. I got into the tub and put a towel under my neck to try to relax. Everything seemed to run in slow motion. Even the water coming out of the faucet slowed and made no sound. Time seemed to stand still. The bath and candles were not helping me to feel better. In fact I was feeling worse. While sitting there, I had another hallucination that Monty came home and stood by the bathtub talking to me. Asking me what was wrong. All I could do to respond was sob and tell him goodbye. Then *poof*! He was gone and I knew he had not come home at all. I was going mad!

I guess I had been in the tub for for about forty-five minutes when I decided I had to find help. I just knew I had to tell someone. This was not me at all. Someone had to understand. I emptied the tub, got dressed, and walked across the street to my neighbor's house. Kurt was standing outside working on the car in the carport. It had just begun to rain. I asked him if Pam was at home. He said, "Yes, she's inside on the computer." He disappeared into the house after I asked him if he could go inside and get her. I stood in the rain crying and pacing in their driveway waiting for her to come out. She didn't come. I felt as if hours had passed. I became frantic. Was the shadow right? Did no one care whether I lived or died? I couldn't stand there any longer. I ran back to our house. I picked up the phone and called my doctor. The secretary answered, so I asked for the doctor's nurse. I was pacing the floor screaming at myself to stop it when the nurse finally came to the phone. I was sobbing again. She tried to calm me and asked me to explain what was wrong. I chose my words carefully knowing that if I said the wrong thing someone would have me committed. I told her that something was wrong. I explained that I was having bad feelings like something was telling me to hurt myself and others. I could not see colors; my brain felt like it was going to explode, I had cysts in my throat and I really felt like it all started after I was given that shot of Lupron. Her response shocked me. She said, "If you felt like that you need to go to the emergency room, we close at noon."

"You're joking," I said.

"No, we cannot help you. We close at noon and if you're feeling that bad then you just need to go to the emergency room."

I couldn't believe my ears. I hung up the phone and went back to pacing. My poor dogs watched over me helplessly. They weren't use to me screaming and crying. I picked up the phone again, this time calling my gynecologist. I told the secretary that it was an emergency. She put me on hold then the nurse finally picked up, and for a second time that day I tried to explain what was happening with me. I reminded her that they had given me the Lupron shot a couple of months ago, and that I was slowly but surely getting sicker. I told her of all the symptoms I was having and asked her if they could help me. She said no. She felt that it was best for me to go straight to the hospital. She felt that they were better equipped to look me over. I told her she had to be kidding and explained that they had given me the shot and I found it difficult to believe that they couldn't help me. This was devastatingly disturbing. She told me that I should call an ambulance or get someone to drive me to the hospital. I hung up. I had no choice; I could either, stay inside the house and let *it* get me, or I fight it. I walked back out into the rain and crossed the street to Kurt's house. I walked up the front steps and knocked on the door. Kurt came and apologized for Pam not coming to out. He noticed that I was crying and asked me what was wrong. I told him I wasn't sure but I needed a ride to the emergency room. I told him I was pretty sure that I was having a bad reaction to the medicine that I had been given by my doctor in December. He almost seemed reluctant to help. I pleaded with him saying that Monty was on a trip and that his mother who lived next to us was in the hospital. I had no one to call and I would not have asked if I didn't think it was important

To say that Kurt was a slow, cautious driver to begin with would be an understatement but I swear it felt like he was driving about ten miles per hour. He parked and came in with me. The nurses checked me in and again, I was very careful about what I said. They told me to have a seat in the lobby and they would call me when they were ready for me. Kurt sat with me for almost ten minutes and then explained that he had to get back to get ready for work. I told him to go ahead, that no matter what happened I would call someone to come get me if the doctor couldn't figure out what was wrong.

I think I only sat there for another fifteen minutes when they called me back. There were two male nurses attending to me. They asked me to explain what was bothering me. I told them about my chest pain, swollen brain, seeing only black and white, and about my extra sensitivity to sound, light, and electronics. They asked me if I was on any type of medication. I started by saying no but then retracted and said yes, revealing that my gynecologist prescribed and injected Lupron in December for endometriosis.

One of the nurses started to groan. "Haven't you heard about that shot?" he asked me.

"No, what should I have heard?"

"My wife was on that medicine and she had gotten a letter in the mail about how bad it was. Didn't you get one?"

"No" I exclaimed.

"Well, we'll try to get you fixed. Come on, we'll take you in to see the doctor."

They put me in a room and tried to make me comfortable.

Why am I telling you all of this? This event tore my life apart and took every bit of four years to get my life back. But the amazing part of the entire mess is that Great Spirit told me before it happened; "Nicole, you will be fine after your near death experience! You must submit to this experience in order to change who you are and where you're going in order to truly live and help others like you." I had no idea what Great Spirit meant at that time. All I remember is that I was shaken from my frame and I thought for sure I was going to die.

The emergency room doctor came, spending a few minutes looking me over. I told him about the medication I had been given and he didn't even flinch when he said, "That is not the issue." The male nurse had more to say to me than this guy! He ordered a CAT scan, a urinalysis and blood work, then left the room to attend to an accident victim that had just been brought in by ambulance.

During this four hour stint I lay curled in a fetal position praying someone would help me before it was too late. At hour marker 3 a mental health professional came in and introduced herself. We chatted for some time about my work and I relayed my concern about telling too many people about it because I figured I'd end up in the psych ward before I could say *boo*. Amazingly she agreed with me. She was still in the room when my results came back. They did not find anything in my urine-which they were checking to see if I was on drugs, the blood work revealed nothing and the CAT scan of my brain came up clean. The nurse left the room after passing on that bit of good news and the mental health consultant turned to me to make a ghastly statement.

"Nicole, you should go home, take two benedryl and go to bed."

I began to cry. "You're kidding?"

"No. If you tell the doctors what you told me, you will be locked up before the days is over. That is my suggestion. Go home and get some rest."

I put my own clothes back on, called my stepdaughter to see if she could pick me up and then waited for the hospital to check me out. After Kelly dropped me off at home I tried all I could to relax. I began wondering what I could do to get some reasonable help. It was not five o'clock yet so I picked up the phone and dialed the gynecologists office again. This time I was sure to ask for the doctor. My regular practitioner was not in but the physicians assistant was there. When she answered the telephone I was quick to suggest she open my records to see that I was given the shot of luprelide acetate. I gave her the high speed low drag version of my hospital jaunt and asked her if that specific drug could cause all of the side effects I had mentioned. To my amazement she said yes! Did I hear her right? I couldn't breathe. I asked her to repeat her answer.

"Yes Nicole, that drug can cause all of those side effects and more but we are not supposed to tell you that."

"So, what am I supposed to do now? Can you get this garbage out of my body?

"No, there is no way to do that," she stated emphatically.

My brain went into overdrive. "Can I get the name of the pharmaceutical company and their phone number from you?"

"Yes, I will put you on hold and the nurse will get back on the line with that information. Now that I have thought about it, we can try something. We can try to counteract the effects of the drug by putting you back on birth control which will put some hormones back in your body."

"Thank you, I may try that but first I think I would like to talk to the pharmaceutical company to see what they have to offer." The PA making that bold statement actually gave me a leg to stand on. I could now find a way to help myself even though I was not really sure how to do it, but I at least felt as if there was a glimmer of hope.

"Nicole?"

"Yes, ma'am."

"The company is TAP Pharmaceutical and here is their number. We are very sorry you are having such a bad reaction to the medicine. Please keep us apprised of the situation."

I thanked her and hung up, only to immediately dial the pharmaceutical company.

Their representative answered the phone cordially but I interrupted her, moving to gain an audience from a nurse or doctor that worked within the company. She told me that the nurse would be right with me and placed me on hold. I paced the floor impatiently like a cat in a room full of rocking chairs and talking to myself the entire time. When the nurse answered I shared my story for what seemed to be the umpteenth time and asked her if there was any way to get the drug out of my system.

"No Nicole, once you have received the injection it will stay in your system for up to three months, at which time you would go back to the doctor to get another injection."

"No way am I going back for another injection. If I were to take another I would surely kill myself. This drug is awful and I need to get it out of me now! Your company made this drug and you are telling me that there is no way to get rid of it?" I had not even caught my breathe when I went on to ask another question. "What is the longest amount of time this drug has stayed in one person's system after only one injection?"

"We are sorry but there is no way. To answer your second question I would have to say a few years, so the only suggestion I can make at this juncture is for you to speak with our risk management office," she concluded.

"Really, and what pray tell do you believe that office will have to tell me that is any differnet than what you have already?

"Well, they are company lawyers and I am sure they will want to know what has happened to you."

"Oh sure they will! Okay, go ahead and forward me to that office. I can't wait to hear what they have to offer."

The phone went silent for a moment and then began to ring. "Good afternoon Nicole, my name is Mr. so and so. I am the pharmaceutical company's attorney. I hear you have had a problem with the drug your physician administered. What can I do to help you?"

"First you can help me get this garbage out of my body. Secondly you can tell me what you are going to do to get this drug off the market if it is causing more harm than good." I can be a little dramatic when I feel as if people's lives are in danger.

"I cannot do either and I want to take this time to tell you that if you were to choose a law suit against us, you will not win. You do not have pockets deep enough to fight us Nicole. There is nothing I can do to help you except to say we are sorry you are not responding well to the treatment."

I hung up. I couldn't take another moment of it. I could not help but feel as if I were doomed. Monty was not home to help me, I could not call on my parents for fear they wouldn't understand, my own attorney was thinking I was on drugs and this shadow thing was trying to get me to kill my husband and myself. There was only one thing left to do. I got down on my hands and knees to pray.

"God, if you mean for me to make it through this night, you are going to have to send help."

By this time I was feeling as if my body was collapsing in on itself. My shoulders and back were hunched, my head was drawn down toward my chest and when looking ahead I could only muster to lift my eyes slightly. Every move I made was excruciatingly painful. As I settled in for a long night I looked at the clock to see how long I would have to endure before dawn. It was only 9 o'clock. Just then the telephone rang. I whinced in pain as I reached for it.

"Nicole, this is Roy. I met you in Charlotte a year ago while you were teaching a class about intuition at Polish Inc. Do you remember me? I was the massage therapist that asked if you could take me on as a student."

"Roy honey, I am sorry but right now I cannot even fight my way out of a wet paper bag. My doctor gave me some medicine and I am not sure I will make it through this night." I believe that what transpired next was only due to an act of God.

"Is there anyone at home with you?"

"No. My husband is out of town and I am alone." Call me crazy, I know but I was not in the frame of mind to worry about whether he as a maniac killer.

"What is your address? I am coming up there!"

Yep, I gave it to him and he drove up from Charlotte in his beat up, oil spewing Honda to save me. I could not believe what was happening. It took him about an hour to get to the house. Upon entering he took one look at me and knew I was not kidding. He began to work on my muscles, trying to relax me and get my hands, arms and legs to release and straighten. As I lay on my massage table God's little angel worked on me for two hours and while he rubbed and stretched my limbs I taught him how to see inside my body.

"Nicole, I see your veins and they all look black, as if you were filled with cancer. I am afraid for you. What else can I do to help?

"I am thinking it will be necessary to drive into Charlotte in the morning to purchase some natural products that have estrogen and other hormones in them. I am not familiar with Charlotte and I cannot drive so would you take me? I will pay you."

"Yes. I can come back in the morning but I am afraid to leave you by yourself. Your heart is beating half out of your chest."

"Okay, let me call my husband and see how he feels about me letting you stay the night in our guest room. That is if you want to do that."

"Yes, I will stay and yes, I will take you to Charlotte. There are a couple of places I am thinking of that will have the products you need."

I got up from the table and called Monty. He answered on the first ring. "Honey, you know I have not been well since I took that shot, right?

He hesitated. "Ye-yes. Why, what's up?"

"Well the side effects got worse and I went to the hospital. They could not help me. I called the gynecologist and they could not help me but did offer some insight into how the drug depletes the body of hormones to squelch the endometrial cysts. The only way I can get what I need is to go to Charlotte tomorrow to get some things from a health store. Honey, I really thought I was a goner but after praying God sent someone to help me. He is here now." I could hear his breathing change. I figured he would freak out but he managed to stay pretty calm.

"Nik, I cannot get home to help you and I wouldn't know what to do anyway, so I will have to let you handle this in any manner you deem necessary. I am sorry but there is nothing I can do."

"Well that's not the first time I have heard that today! I am going to let Roy Hatcher stay the night in our guest room. He does not have enough fuel in his car to get back to Charlotte tonight and he feels as if someone needs to be here with me. Are you okay with this?"

"I guess I have no other choice. Do what you need to and we will talk tomorrow."

I showed Roy to the guest room and said goodnight. I hoped he would be okay, afterall, we did not know each other very well and he was in a strange home with two dogs that did not know him; one of which was a retired police dog that was extremely protective of me when Monty was not at home.

I sat rocking on the edge of my bed without sleeping. The pain in my chest was outrageous and my heart would not relax for even a minute. I stared at the clock praying for daylight and as soon as I saw a glimmer of it coming through the bedroom curtains I changed my clothes, woke Roy and we began our trek south, into the city.

He took me to two places. Each had just what I needed to realkalize my body. My body was totally acidic which is what caused the cysts in my throat. To decrease the acid and boost alkalinity I needed liquid chlorophyll in order to impact on the body fast. Then I needed products that would provide some natural hormones. I opted for the simplest and easiest thing I could get my hands on which, in this instance happened to be extra strength *Estroven*,[1] *Calms Forte* [2]to help my body relax, and *Rescue Remedy* [3]to further soothe my nerves, organic chlorophyll to create a more alkaline environment within my body, potassium, calcium, magnesium and much more. The second store had a juice bar so I had them mix me up a fruit and veggie smoothie and I added all of my products to the drink. Fifteen minutes later, as Roy and I were heading back north toward Kannapolis I actually began to feel better. After returning home I surfed the internet and ordered an oral chelating agent to remove the medication from my bloodstream, which is what I believe quickened my healing processes. Now, although I mention these products here I must also suggest that you not self medicate if you are experiencing ill effects from medication you are presently taking. The day after I began taking these natural remedies I called my general practitioner and had a meeting with her to discuss exactly what I was doing and asked her to take this journey with me. I reiterate, this is not something you should do alone.

As for Roy, I can honestly say that he saved my life that night. I do not believe I would have been strong enough to fight off the shadow man. Since he showed up in my life one year after seeing him at that one class I had taught, I can only surmise that God knew I was in trouble and meant for me to make it through the ordeal.

So what happened after that? Well, I joined a Lupron victims support group on *Yahoo* and shared everything I did to get better. I shared my letters to the pharmaceutical company, the hospital and my doctors. I left no stone unturned when I found out that doctors were prescribing luprelide acetate to children for precocious puberty. The parents of those poor children were beside themselves trying to figure out how to save their kids. If what I did could do the same thing for their children this was the least I could do. It was almost one year from the date Spirit told me I would be fine after my near death experience and that I was to share that experience with others so they too could heal.

It took every bit of four years for me to get my life back and get the medication out of my body. No help from the pharmaceutical company, of which merged with Takeda Pharmaceuticals to form one of the top fifteen pharmaceutical companies in the United States. The merger was the result of their thirty-year joint venture, but interestingly Takeda received rights to more specific products of which were non-Lupron related. Effective May 1, 2008, TAP would no longer exist as a separate entity reporting to Takeda America Holdings Inc. When I found out about the merger I called them to see if they would do anything to help those other people that were adversely affected by the medication, and their attorney scoffed at me and nonchalantly stated that I could not pursue a lawsuit against them.

Now I know why I am here. This is part of the reason I am writing this book. It's not for me to dump all of this *stuff* on paper to get it all out of my mind. This book is for you. To show you how precious life really is, to tell you that this time that we are living in is sacred. This is the time for all of us to start taking responsibility for our own thoughts and actions; to realize that we had given our power away to our politicians, doctors, and businessmen. Was it up to them to fix our lives, make us better by healing our bodies, make us wealthy, or just the opposite—ruin our lives, take away things we worked hard for? What I have come to learn by my experiences is that we have more power to do all these things than we have given ourselves credit for. We chose the fast food, fast fixes, fast doctors that give us seven minutes of their time and a prescription for what ails us. We could sit back and blame them but we can't because we are willing participants and we chose it all. Good, bad, or otherwise, we allowed others to provide us with the tools to self-destruct.

So where do we go from here? What does our personal *sacred time* look like? Yours may have a different story line, but in the thick of it, all of our stories will be similar in nature; merging or overlapping in some instances. Our true essence as a divine spirit in human form will have similar traits.

- We all want a lifetime of perfect health and longevity.

- We all want more wealth than we'll ever need or maybe just have enough to be comfortable. Security and safety.

- We all want to have a purpose.

- We all want to belong to something, to be wanted, loved, and remembered.

- We all want a rewarding career and success

I think we all aspire to be more than we are and why wouldn't we. The human body, mind and spirit are extraordinary and should be shared with others.

I began this book by sharing some of my life experiences with you, which I will continue to do. In doing so I have all ideas that you will begin to allow your life's experiences to resurface within you after years of stagnation and...you too will have some profound moments and rationalizations just as I had. I have had years to research just how our bodies try to communicate with us. How aches and pains we try to suppress every day are merely our bodies way of trying to get us to *pay attention*.

In order to understand, we need to look at the *child* that we once were. As I write I will call on my inner child *Nikki*. Nikki shows herself to me as she would be at four years old, she loves animals and trusts everything and everyone. She believes that all creatures are inherently good. One day while taking a walk through her neighborhood to see a lady friend, she encounters a bumblebee. She steps up onto her friend's doorstep and a bumblebee begins to fly around her little hand. Instead of swatting at the bee she opens her hand and produces her pointer finger for the bee to land on. She admires its beauty with delight as it lands and begins to crawl around. And in an instant this beautiful serene picture changes to terror and bewilderment. That beautiful creature, without any provocation, stung her! Just then her lady friend opened the door to find Nikki screaming as her tears poured from her beautiful brown eyes. She dances around in place, shaking her hand trying to dislodge the stinger. Then as her lady friend tried to comfort her, Nikki took off in a gallop toward her home for comfort and security. She could not believe that something so wonderful could be so mean and hurtful. After all, she had done nothing to hurt the bee.

Innocence! As children, we trust. We trust until something happens that makes us close our hearts and build walls around our emotions. If this would have happened to Nikki as an adult, she would have rationalized the entire episode. She would not have been so hurt by the little bee turning on her as thoughts about the true nature of any creature are just a reasonable rationalization.

I still, to this day, find myself looking for bees in the garden so I can pet them. My husband, stepdaughter, and mother-in-law think I'm crazy. On many occasions, Ida and I have sat outside talking near her rose and herb garden. While engaged in an idle chit chat with her I found that I became fixated on the bees pollinating the flowers, and I can't help myself. I would get up while having the conversation with Ida and stick my finger out to let the big bumble bees land on me. I love to feel their soft pollen covered hair. I wouldn't push my weight down on them, or make them feel that they were in danger.I merely touched them with love in my heart, appreciating them. Have I thought about whether they were capable of hurting me? Of course I have, but I am not scared anymore. Here is the important thing to keep in mind as you create what it is you want in life. Within my sacred time and space I am part of everything that exists therefore my true essence permeates the cells of anything within my environment. I'll say it another way; there is nothing in my body, or being, that has the *want* to hurt anything around me. Therefore, as I interact with my environment, nothing within my environment *wants* to hurt me. How do you learn to interact with your environment like this? Keep reading.

Tapping the Power Within

MY INTENTION WAS to write this book in such a way that anyone, of any stature, could read and understand it. I had started pulling all of my journals together and writing in September of 2005, one year after I had awakened from my four year, chemically induced slumber. Although I knew God and believed in him before my horrifying experiences with the medication I think my connection to the source intensified more so during and after the four year journey. I value my existence and feel strongly that I would not be here to share my story unless there was a higher power guiding me to do so. I am far from perfect, but I strive to do right—to leave everything I touch in better condition than the way I found it. As an Empath (a feeling person), I care and feel more deeply about others than I care to admit sometimes, but I know to the depths of my soul that the degree at which I *feel* is only due to my connectedness to God,

Jesus Christ, and the Holy Spirit. The gifts God provided upon my birth have lead me to fulfill my destiny.

When I was a child, my grandfather told me a story about our family's Native American heritage; suggesting that we had Native American blood running through our veins. Whether it was true or not, I believed him and it was my perception of his story that led me to study herbs, homeopathic and complementary medicine. I love the earth and its extraordinary ability to adapt and overcome cataclysmic events. I have valued my connectedness to all life forms and due to my perception of these things I believe my life story played out as it has. I trust that it was my relationship with God that saved my life and I am thankful for each day I have to share what I have gleaned from my experiences. You will harvest the information that you are supposed to from the pages of this book in order to put them into practice. Whether you use them now or merely remember them when all else fails. These tools will shift your life from ordinary to extraordinary and it will lead you to become your own best advocate, doctor, or caregiver to others in the coming years.

Post–Lupron:
My Inner God Revealed

JANUARY 2008, WYATT; my bigheaded English Lab lay sleeping at my feet while I reread *Spirit Song*, a book written by Mary Summer Rain, an empathically gifted student of No-Eyes, a Native American shaman and visionary. I earmarked a page as I neared the end of the book and turned my attention to thinking about how God gave the people the truth about everything. He gave us free will and endowed us with guides and teachers that would help us along our life journey no matter the circumstances. Through cataclysmic and meteorological conditions humanity has been tested, and will continue to be. Does God control these events? I am not sure we can be certain about that but it does bring a memory to mind. While visiting a healing facility in Virginia our group encountered a pretty significant rainstorm. As we toured the property a member of the group asked if I thought we could stop the rain merely by focusing on it. So we did. The five or so that were in the group stood focusing our energy on clearing the storm clouds and telling the rain to stop and within minutes it actually did. As the sun came out around us and the rain cleared we looked around at one another and began laughing. We wondered how long it would take to start raining again so instead of getting stuck outside in another downpour we headed back into the building. As we got resettled inside the pelting rain began again. That raises another question. Can we control the weather? To some extent, through focus and intention I think we can. That also raises yet another question. Is the weather affected by our moods or unrelenting injustices? I cannot be sure just yet but something tells me that even the tides are affected by the decisions we make, how we treat one another and are also connected to how we feel about life. Interestingly cataclysmic events have transpired more over the past twenty years or so and seem to be happening at an accelerated rate.

As I chewed on my thoughts I looked back at the book. Even No-Eyes felt as if people have had ample warning and I would have to agree. We have all had plenty of time to change our ways and believe in something larger or more grand than ourselves. Crazy at it seems, people tend to not change until they are directly affected by something that forces them to change. Those that choose to walk the same old beaten path and do nothing for the betterment of humanity will either come around or not. I am not here to sit in judgment over anyone; I am merely watching and paying attention. I am mindful and getting ready to act in alignment with whatever comes.

Interestingly, thinking about such things brought something else to mind so I turned to the first pages of Summer's book to look at the date of publishing. Summer published her book *Spirit Song* in 1985 around the same time that the Hopi Indians came out with a documentary called *Earth Changes*, predicting many natural and catastrophic events for our planet. The Hopi Indians also forewarned us about changing our ways so that we would survive and be able to carry on even in the toughest of times.

Just in case you had not noticed, there are many more of us on the *change bandwagon* these days. I think many more people now know deep within our hearts that things cannot continue the way they had in the past. We have an inner knowing that we all must adapt to the changes that are taking place and adopt new behaviors in order to create a more peaceful space for the generations to come. Having presented this, I also have to say that there are many young spirits-new to the body and earth experience-that do not want to, nor do they feel they should, change. If you were to research Mary Summer Rain and No Eyes you might stumble upon forums that suggest that Summer Rain is a fraud. We tend to see this happening when someone does not agree with another person. Instead of just letting people have their own opinion they feel they must belittle or berate the ones they disagree with. Interestingly when I experience others acting in this manner, I feel sick to my stomach. Not that I am judging their act but rather, my body translates their act as hurtful and it affects my body adversely. Some people want so badly to be heard; to make their point; that they don't realize how hurtful they are being. I disagree with those that think Summer Rain is a fraud. This is my prerogative, just as it is your right to believe the way you do. If you do not like her books...I might suggest that you not purchase them but keep in mind-you were drawn to pick them up and buy them for some reason and that may have more to do with the universal consciousness (God source) putting them in your path to initiate change so that you and those around you can benefit by something that author had to offer.

Just as Mary Summer Rain was directed to write her books, I was directed to write this first book to assist in the prevention of disease, in the healing and rebalancing of the body, and the shifting of our consciousness so that we can teach the coming generations to be more empathetic and proactive as the Earth shifts. In the event something should transpire, where you are unable find the expertise or resourceful individuals you think you need, the techniques within these pages will provide you with the confidence that is essential to handle whatever may come. Keep in mind that learned behavior, societal stresses, and our own self-driven ways have led many of us to forget that we came into this life pure, with a connection to a universal cache—the God source—which is a divine reserve overflowing with resources and answers to our many questions; answers to every question we could ever have in one lifetime.

I believe that No-Eyes and Mary Summer Rain knew this to be true and that they willingly submitted to sharing their heritage, their lives, their spiritual wisdom, and the great mysteries that are stored within each living thing on this planet. They sought to teach us how truly extraordinary we are and that the God source within ourselves would lead to a never-ending wealth of information that would change the face of humanity, thereby creating a more empathic society void of slaughter and destruction.

Intrigued with the idea that we do not have to allow ourselves to become a product of our environment, I began to look for others that had similar thoughts and ideas about how we might take better care of ourselves. I also wanted to be sure I addressed the idea of being cut off from key resources in the wake of disaster; chief resources being medical doctors, food supply chains, and other people.

> "The doctor of the future would give no medicine, but would interest his patients in the care of the human frame, in diet, and in the cause and prevention of disease."
>
> —Thomas Edison

As visions flooded my minds-eye revealing the misfortunes of those entangled in recent natural disasters, my thoughts were interrupted. I turned my attention inward questioningly. Holding my intent for an answer to the possibility of such instability, my inner God-source brought my awareness to rest upon visionary Thomas Edison (1847–1931). He proclaimed that

"The doctor of the future would give no medicine, but would interest his patients in the care of the human frame, in diet, and in the cause and prevention of disease." One could safely assume that he knew something was wrong with the way his fellow men and women were caring for themselves—even back then. The origin of this quote was a notion claimed for the Health Maintenance Organization (HMO) relating a concept that has dominated the U.S. medical industry over the past few decades. This is an industry which would provide prepaid medical services to people for a set fee, encouraging them to seek preventative or early care. and take responsibility for their own health. It was thought that this method would head off hefty costs associated with serious illness and hospitalization. That concept was not practiced until the 1970s but amazingly, it is a concept physician's and medical institutions are now trying to move toward changing due to the realization that the old system of healthcare is not working for the masses. Many tend to wait until their conditions are extreme before seeking care. Countless individuals believe that their physician knows them better than they know themselves which can be a grave mistake because many organizations that employ physicians only allow under ten minutes, (typically 4–7 minutes), with each patient to diagnose and treat them. How is it possible for a physician to digest your entire history in ten minutes or less?

Edison was not a mad man, but rather, a man that could foresee the future; a future where individuals would have to be aware of their doings and participate in their care.

Let's be realistic. As you look at your environment and our economy, what do you see? You can see that we are all being pushed into a proverbial corner. We are at a place where it has become necessary to fix what is broken or leave the broken bits behind; to adapt, overcome and be more attentive to our environment, one another and ourselves. Intuitively, I don't feel that it's possible to totally destroy the human race, although the evolution of our race has revealed our propensity or susceptibility toward such an occurrence. Edison felt that the *patching up* of the sick man was coming to an end in his lifetime, thereby opening the door to a focus of preventative medicine. It has taken eighty-two years for this idea to take hold. During what I consider to be the climax period of human existence, humanity spent a great deal of energy around creating war trappings but, declared that they were doing it in the name of peace. I have to say, who needs war when we are being inundated with pollutants that can destroy us from within. This includes the things we ingest and all of the stimuli we encounter that assaults the cells of our bodies. The overload of multiple layers of toxicity requires a fracturing, or fundamental shift in perception. We need to recognize that what most of us are in search of does not come from outside of ourselves, but rather, from within.

Poet Ymber Delecto suggested that *a healthy body and soul come from an unencumbered mind and body*. Think about all of the things we encounter and do in a day's time. Most of us are stressed to the max, wondering where our next paycheck will be coming from or how we will pay for our food, childcare, or medical insurance. Talk about overloaded! How many people do you know that aren't worried about something? I can't think of one. Even with the best of intentions, I get so caught up in my work and wanting things to turn out exactly as I planned that I forget to stay centered. Due to years of research and personal application of these processes, I can now offer up an extraordinary revelation that personally took years to embrace. Even in the grimmest of situations the body has its own rebalancing tools. All we need to do is tap into this power and use it. When anxiety grips you and pain shoots through your body, know that the cells in your body hold the key to restoration. To rebalance and heal you will first need to understand what your body is trying to tell you. So it is through subtle or severe pain signals the mind and body is actually communicating its likes and displeasures to us every second of the day—sending out warning signals, quite like an internal distress signal—a Morse code, if you will. By becoming innately aware of the signals we can lighten our emotional loads and inspire divine order within our bodies and, with practice, we can then begin to reach out into our external world. We can touch the lives of others by utilizing this virtual link between our inner body and our intellectual God mind or God-source, which is connect to all other things. Our Native American Elders were intimately familiar with the philosophy around being connected to everything and it stands to reason that we should get back in alignment with this rationale.

Consider the number of people on this planet. With this concept of tapping onto our innate God-source wisdom, I am suggesting that it is possible to unfetter any community mind to spark change that will create a healthy community body, and expand outward to create peace on this planet. Holding my intention on hearing the truthful answer to this question I turn within—into my own body—to tap into my cells and ask my inner God-source. It felt as if the hands of God cradled me and supported this truth; my organs vibrating in answer to a new, uncompromising reality. Will this happen in my lifetime? Maybe not, but that won't stop me from holding the intention of creating this type energy within my own community.

Alison Rose Levy, the author of *An Ancient Cure for Modern Life* wrote: "In minds crammed with thoughts, organs clogged with toxins, and bodies stiffened with neglect, there is just no space for anything else."

Life is a never-ending matrix; a vast network of free flowing energy that supports all things. This complex network is sustained by the God source to include all that exists within the human body, as well as all of the endless outside stimuli that bombards us every minute of each day.

First Corinthians 3:16 reads, "Don't you know that you yourselves are God's temple and that God's Spirit lives in you?" My understanding of this is that God resides in each of us. Some scientists might prefer a different perspective but quantum physics sheds new light on the idea of the Godhead and its connection to humanity.

University of Oregon physicist, Amit Goswami wrote *God is Not Dead*, which suggests that there is a feeling that we get that provides the first sign of something beyond the physical plane and moves us to and that leads us to deliberate on the spiritual. Feeling is, by far, left unexplained by science. Goswami further expressed it thus:

> When we look at our experiences of feeling, meaning, and the archetypal contexts of feeling and meaning through the conceptual lens of the new science—science within consciousness—we find that there is ample experimental proof that they don't arise from the physical body. They occur in conjunction with the body, but they are not the physical body. Instead they come from God, or more accurately from the Godhead; we choose them from our own God potential. In other words, no mystic has to tell us that God is our *father*. Every one of us has that intuition already. The new science is just validating that intuition.

Moreover, he stated: "The God hypothesis is needed to incorporate feelings as part of our experience. You will notice that feeling-oriented cultures tend to be believers in God (good or bad), whereas when rationalism dominates a culture, it tends to move away from the God hypothesis. This is not a coincidence." (page 153)

The exercise of choice is God's exercise of the power of downward causation or action. Are we, individually, responsible for the things we take in, as well as that energy which we send back out into the world?

Goswami contends that it is consciousness, not matter that is the ground of all existence; maintaining that the universe is self-aware (we do not have to give that any thought— it exists without us putting energy into it), and that our consciousness creates the physical world.

When we are busy living in fear, worrying about how we are going to feed our families and take care of ourselves, we are not consciously thinking about what we can do to help others. Better still, when in this state we may not be receptive to tapping into the resources that are left untainted within us that can be readily shared for the betterment of mankind.

In conclusion, the information passed down from generation to generation yields great wisdom for those of us that seek enlightenment, a path to perfect health and even world peace. Those that feel pressured only to succeed or simply survive the trying times take no pleasure in straying away from their self-driven ways in order to find a better way, tranquility or peace that could ultimately change the way they live from day to day. Years of toxins, negativity and ego based thinking brings us to where we stand today. We are in toxic overload! Fast food, being over medicated, too much stimuli, lusting after outcomes, and our fear based thinking leaves our bodies in a state of perpetual inequity.

Questions like: Where do we go from here?, How can we make a difference in our own lives as well as the lives of others?, and How do we stop the senseless killing, the over consumption, the overmedicating and the fear based living? My answer to you is quite simply, *we tap the power within.*

> "Respect and appreciate that you are the only you that will ever be here in this particular time and place; for in one second, you will be changed forever." (Nicole Myers Henderson)

My Purpose

I WAS IN MY early twenties when I began asking my body questions, but I was not moved to do any major introspection until 2003, just after I had found out that I had endometriosis. I had gotten married in 1999 and as most of you know, when you marry someone with children and you have none of your own the relationship tends to mutate once you say the words *I do*. My stepdaughter was rebelling against me, and I began to feel unappreciated and disrespected. Each time I tried to talk to my husband about how I felt the tables were turned on me and I would ultimately be accused of hating her and not wanting her in our lives. That wasn't me at all. I can't ever remember ever hating anything. So I held my feelings in until my body couldn't take it any longer.

Perception of our experiences and memories, as well as our judgments of them affects the biological activity of our body. Negative and positive stimulation from

our external environment impinges on sensory recep-
tors and in turn produce neural activity sending signals
to organs and systems to either cause it to build up or
break down. This is one explanation for illness manifesting within the physical body.

Two years into our marriage I began having abdominal pain. I remember it to be excruciating, and I ended
up visiting my doctor many times to discuss my options.
Doc would ask questions like: What's going on at
home? Are you happy? Is something upsetting you? For
the life of me, I couldn't attribute my aches and pains to
my emotional state because the pain was purely physical. Each time I spoke to her about it, her only solution
was to put me on antidepressants and do nothing about
the abdominal pain. I found myself growing angry and
strongly objecting to her solution. I kept telling her that
it was definitely pain and that I knew my body better
than she did, but she would not listen-she didn't and
she wouldn't. She was the professional and she knew
better. So, after much rebellion, introspection, and feeling as if I had no other options I submitted to her line
of thinking. If I was depressed and this wasn't physical
pain, the meds might actually help.

Now, for those of you that have tried antidepressants, you probably know how they make you feel. We
had to try a few different types because of side effects.
I had adverse reactions to a number of them until we
found one that did not make me feel like a zombie.
Although with all of them, I felt as if I was wearing a
mask that would never allow me to smile. The one we
finally settled on also came with side effects, like the

others, but they were not as extreme. It worked only in that it made me feel like I didn't care about the pain so much. I felt broken, and I didn't care to interact with anyone. Every so often, I would feel as if my head was stuffed under the Liberty Bell while someone struck its hard exterior with a sledge hammer. It felt like the chugging noise was going to turn my innards to mush and the abdominal pain never went away. Even after two years on the meds my body tried to show me that there was something very wrong inside. Because I was not getting any relief, my body continued to signal for help and the side effects intensified.

I revisited my doctor, stressing my feelings about the pain and told her that I knew this was a physical issue. I was relieved when she finally admitted she did not know what it was and willingly suggested I go see a gynecologist to get an ultrasound.

My gynecologist did the ultrasound and found that I had been plagued by a ovarian cyst. She took me off of the antidepressants and suggested I take my birth control pills in such a way as to make my body think it was in menopause. This meant that I was to take my twenty-eight day cycle of pills but move to a new pack without taking the period pills. Acting in this manner would give my body a break and keep from having inner bleeding that was causing the cysts to grow and spread. I definitely felt a difference but I was still afflicted with pain. The doctor suggested surgery on a few occasions but I was unwilling to submit due to my body's distaste of anesthesia. After much pain and contemplation, I submitted to surgery to have the ovarian cyst removed.

Months after surgery, I was still experiencing abdominal pain so I went back to my doctor to discuss my options. *Mental note: I think we forget that our physical body takes years to break down, and we most often think that the body should be able to heal very quickly.* My doctor suggested that I take a shot that would essentially throw me into menopause and stop my body from making cysts completely. Interestingly, images of doctor's visits from my childhood surfaced and tugged at my brain. I just didn't feel right about this so I told her I needed time to think it over.

I became quite compulsive about my health and began praying for God to help me make this decision. I didn't feel like I could trust anyone to help me with this decision due to the number of disappointments I had experienced in regard to my healthcare previously. I wasn't even sure I could trust myself to know what was best, because I had been prone to making poor decisions in allowing people into my life who ultimately hurt me or let me down in the past.

I remember contemplating the reasons behind my behavior and wondered what my trigger was. It seemed odd that I was intuitively being pulled to look at an event that could have sparked this type of conduct. I was not clear on my intention, but I felt inclined to let this line of thinking play itself out. As I held my focus on the possible reasons, and almost spontaneously, in answer to my inner probing, my body showed me a very meaningful conversation my father had with me when I was about four years old. This was amazing! It was as if I was back there reliving it. I was watching my child self-interacting with my father one morning that he had stayed home from work.

He said that he was going to hang out with me. It may have been due to the fact that my mother was working, or quite possibly because he had nothing better to do. Either way, it wasn't often that he stayed home or hung out with me. I remembered feeling a sense of excitement as he chose to share his valuable time with me. It made me feel special.

Here we are-home alone. He begins by telling me that he is going to teach me how to make my bed. As I view images of the memory, I am amazed that I can also hear my child-self thinking, *Yeah! Daddy is going to hang out with me today. This is going to be so much fun!* The memory plays out in my mind's eye as if I was right there reliving it again.

Dad leads me to the bedroom and proceeds to pull all of the covers off of my bed. I see my child-self writhing with excitement. He begins the lesson by explaining: "It is important that you always leave something looking better than the way you found it, Nicole." He performed the bed-making dance to perfection, showing me how to tuck in the corners and make the sheets as tight as possible. He capped it off with my favorite quilt and pillow.

My child-self was laughing and dancing about with joy, like a racehorse prancing at the starting gate, ready to get to work. She was barely able to contain herself. All she wanted to do was show him that she could make it look just as pretty as when he did it.

As he went into the other room, she made the bed precisely as he had—or so she thought. She finished with the quilt and rushed out to get him. As he walked into the bedroom I, the adult-self that was watching the memory play out, could tell straight away that he disapproved of her work. As he tore the bed apart he told her that it looked okay, but he was going to show her how to do it again. I could see the little girl within, crouching down, slinking back into her shell, feeling crushed. She waited-wondering if she could do it right the next time.

As my adult self stood there watching the memory replay, I found that I was thinking about how cruel he was being to her. To my surprise, she heard my thoughts. Wide-eyed she peered up at me and addressed me by saying, "I have been left in here to deal with this mess. You abandoned me, so you have no right to talk about how cruel he's being to me!" She was angry! At me! What did I do to her? I didn't even know I could experience these things until this happened. I was taken aback by her anger, but it began to register in my brain that if I was going to find answers regarding this process, and why it was happening, I would have to make friends with her and show her that she was safe with me.

As if hearing all of my thoughts, she went back to showing me the filmstrip-like memory.

Dad finished pulling the covers back off the bed and walked from the room. I saw my child-self begin the bed-making process again. This time she made sure the sheets were tight. She climbed on the bed and smoothed them out with both arms, then climbed down to pull them tighter, topping it off with the quilt to cover the pillows. When she finished, she stood back to survey her work, then looked at me to see if I approved. I looked at her, she looked at me, and we both shrugged. This time she seemed more dissatisfied by her efforts but figured she would have to let him have the final say.

Dad followed her into the room again, this time seeming a bit short tempered and snide. With one flip of his wrist, he pulled all the covers off the bed again. This time he did not remake the bed. He stood back and said that she would have to keep doing it until she got it right. I watched in amazement as the two of them went through the motions of bed making a few more times. She tried and tried but could not please him.

I was saddened by her unsuccessful efforts. I felt crushed all over again. I could hear her mumbling under her breath, "If this is how it feels to spend time together, he can just go back to work!"

She was fed up, and through this experience she came to learn that Dad staying home meant hard work and no play.

It was interesting how the memory helped me understand why I try to do things right the first time through. Why I feel as if there is no sense in doing anything half-heartedly, which would only lead me to have to do things again and again.

My body giving me the answer to my question intrigued me and offered a fresh perspective that would prove to be a perfect internal guidance system that would be accessible day or night. Through many years of self-work and practicing these techniques with my clients, I have come to realize that we all have this ability. At first it did not seem natural. Clients have said the same thing, but once they try it, they feel the difference. Their pain or illness just goes away, as if it had never been there short of them having the conscious memory of the time lost being in that state of discomfort.

The days come and go. I feel normal, living life and experiencing things as most do. The only difference is that I am hardwired in to each person I meet. At times, I am able to grasp the enormity of the gift God entrusted me with; a gift that allows me to feel what others feel, see what others see, and experiencing things that most people have only ever day dreamed about. I always have to be mindful of what I am feeling–Are my feelings my own or someone else's. Being empathic allows me to walk a thousand miles in someone else's shoes, and at times, I need a reminder that what I am feeling does not always belong to me. We each have this to some degree, and many choose to ignore what they feel, while others get caught up in thinking that what they feel is related to them and their body rather than it coming from outside of them.

Today, human awareness has shifted leaving more and more people to realize that their gut feelings are not so easy to dismiss. Interestingly, the skills I have mastered began with seeing ghosts when I was four years old. It still freaks me out when I sense them but I have learned to ask questions and guide them as it becomes necessary. I remember receiving criticism from my aunt Catherine about sharing such experiences with others as a child. They said that no one wanted to hear about those things and that others would not understand. I discovered, after receiving some distasteful looks, that rather than speak about the experiences, it was easier to retreat to hang out with my animal friends. They didn't judge or criticize me. They loved me for being with them and I found that they were far easier to please and more trustworthy than most people. I spent much of my life sidestepping and shying away from people. My perception of those hurtful experiences shadowed my true path in life and it took many years for me to fully accept and love this facet of myself. I realized that I expended enormous amounts of energy on not wanting to feel vulnerable to people, creating a story that only gave me a false sense of security. I heard myself telling others how I longed to grow up to work with animals; to be a veterinarian; knowing full well that I was only masking my feelings of insecurity. I knew that I was choosing to hide behind my love of animals because I did not want to dwell on my feelings of vulnerability, nor subject myself to the callousness and expectations of others.

Purposeful Combined Effort

AS A TEENAGER, I was fascinated by the growth of trees and plants. You cut off a limb, branch, or stem and another would grow back. Even in my youth, I felt sure that since trees and plants could regenerate, scientists would soon discover how our cells could do the same thing.

Now as I write, my body reveals a memory of a conversation I had with a friend. He had been experiencing heart problems. The heart specialist informed him that one of the main arteries into his heart had withered and died but fortunately the body was already creating more. After revisiting the memory of that particular conversation, I chose to do a bit more digging to see any other scientific progress had been made in regard to cellular or organ regeneration.

Dr. Charles Vacanti and colleagues in the Department of Anesthesiology at UMass Medical

Center in Worcester, Massachusetts created what became known as the *earmouse*. The Vacanti mouse, or earmouse as they called it, was a laboratory mouse that looked as if a human ear was growing on its back. The *ear* was an ear-shaped cartilage structure grown by seeding cow cartilage cells into a biodegradable ear-shaped mold and then implanted under the skin of the mouse. Although, no genetic engineering was involved in making the ear, the photos passed around the internet in the nineties created a stir of protest. This was interesting, but I needed something more to sink my teeth into.

Ah, here we go-the liver! "The human liver is one of the few organs in the body that can regenerate from as little as 25 percent of its tissue," says Seth Karp, main study author and assistant professor of surgery at Harvard Medical School in Boston. Karp also suggests that organ regeneration has also been observed in animals although details pertaining to how it happens at a cellular level have yet to be determined.

An article I had read in 2007 indicates that there are proteins involved that induce organ regeneration which have been identified and scientists aim to re-grow organs by stimulating these proteins. Imagine how this would change the lives of veterans that had lost limbs during war, benefit children that are being born without appendages, or transform the lives of burn victims.

Scientists are digging into complicated matters and the exploration of new and better treatments are being developed and employed each day, but what if we were to give our body what it needs—will it regenerate cells on its own? To answer this question, let us expound further upon the idea of liver regeneration. I will act as the subject in order to convey an idea. Mind you, this is just an example and I do not have liver damage. If my physician had performed a liver function test and determined that a deficiency existed, I would utilize the techniques I teach regarding cellular communication and request that the liver tell me what it needs in order to heal. Without interference from my conscious mind, my liver would offer insight about eating more beets. By doing so, the body could then stimulate the cells within the liver and it would tell me that it will heal itself. If I did not understand why my body suggested beets I would do some research before adding them to my diet. Upon further investigation, I discovered one of the world's leading authorities on natural healing; Dr. David Williams, a medical researcher, biochemist, and chiropractor that traveled the world uncovering natural treatments and cures for practically every major health concern determined that beets are rich in betaine. In his web article "Beets Can't Be Beaten," Dr. Williams reveals that beets rich in betaine stimulate liver cell function and provide a protective effect for the liver and bile ducts. One recent study found that ingesting beets can also have a significant tumor-inhibiting effect and may help to prevent cancer. Another benefit of betaine is its ability to reduce homocysteine levels— the toxic amino acid that increases your risk of cardiovascular disease. In this instance, I must also add that you should not begin adding anything to your diet that you do not already eat until you have spoken to your physician first because beets are also a source of oxalates, a chemical found in plants, animals and humans, which can concentrate in the kidney and lead to stone formations in certain high-risk individuals. For those at risk of developing kidney stones or those that have gallbladder problems, experts suggest eating less oxalate-containing foods such as beet or beet juice.

This investigative process as well as my curiosity brought me back full circle. Just when had I begun to seek answers to my attraction to the growth and death cycles of cells? In response to my question, my body took me back nineteen years when I began studying the effects of herbs, homeopathies, and botanicals. I consumed information ravenously in an effort to help others understand and be more open to alternative health treatments just in case they found themselves in a place where they were uncomfortable or dissatisfied with modern medical treatments. Author Nancy Gordon, PhD offers that, the lens through which we choose to see ourselves and the world determines the outcome. If we were to look at the three-dimensional body without first putting on our 3-D glasses, we would only see pieces and parts of the whole—not the whole. We will *see things in isolation and never grasp the whole picture.* Modern-day physicist David Bohm observes that the *separation of mind and body* are key issues and challenges that face the Western world. Bohm substantiates that mind and matter are the same thing—energy. As Gordon states in her book, *The Guiding Philosophy for the Future of Healthcare*: "Western medicine has made tremendous strides in understanding the technical side of many conditions; however, what has not been as clearly understood is the question of how our thoughts, emotions, beliefs, and perceptions enhance and maintain health, or not." She purposes that: "just about every challenge we face in Western medicine is related to this perceived separation in some way." In order to transcend the old paradigm of care, we will individually need to do our part and become more familiar with our own lives rather than expect someone else to do our work for us.

It is to this end that I share the technique of cellular memory detoxification so that you can apply them to your life in order to find clarity, peace and healing. By developing the ability to explore emotions and memories stored within your cellular makeup, you will be able to detoxify old outmoded ideas, perceptions and experiences that are not healthy for you and, you will become proficient at tapping into your innate God-source for answers to all of your life questions.

Now, more than ever before, we see powerful thinkers presenting the world with tools and techniques that can aid and educate us, not only discovering our true nature but also, in the profound healing that takes place within the human body on a cellular level.

Deepak Chopra and Andrew Weil have written extensively on the body's infinite ability to change and heal.

Dr. Norm Shealy, M.D., Ph.D., founding president of the American Holistic Medical Association articulates, "*We don't even have to know how the body needs to do the healing. All we have to do is breathe, meditate, and channel life force energy from the earth through our own bodies. The body's intelligence system knows what needs to be healed and the energy will go there!"*

Nancy Gordon, PhD, suggests that our universe is an expanding universe—*what we focus on expands*, and we are limited only by our thoughts and beliefs.

If our focus is on being more connected to our body it will be as simple as we allow it to be. I pose the question, what if we focus on taking responsibility for our health and well-being, and became our own best advocate? We choose not to give away our power to anyone for any reason; we know ourselves inside and out, we choose not to pour all of our hope into our healthcare practitioners but instead hold ourselves accountable for it all. By tapping into our God-source we learn to trust our body, we allow IT to guide us and we choose to be mindful of its wants and needs in order to keep it functioning at peak capacity. By trusting in the innate God-source and its submissions, we can then use the information provided to guide our physicians if we encounter an issue that the body says it cannot heal on its own.

Most of us are guilty of wanting the fastest way to relief and the easiest road to our objective. Do we really need to experience disorder and disease? Do we have to be humbled time and time again before we realize that it is our responsibility to temper our actions and strive to create order and peace within our own lives instead of looking to people and things outside of ourselves for answers? What will you do in the event of a physician shortage?

AARP's Bulletin, Real Possibilities issue, March 2013 article on *How to Beat the Doctor Shortage* reveals that the population is aging, so *there's a greater need for primary care physicians, physicians are getting older, internists are choosing not to accept Medicare patients,* and *primary doctors are in such demand that they choose not to accept Medicare-whose reimbursements to physicians are lower than private insurance rates* and the shortage of doctors is much worse than people might think. A survey performed in 2012 by the Physicians foundation reported that 830,000 physicians are over the age of 50 and seeing fewer patients than they did four years ago.

The Affordable Care act ushers in new challenges. Russell Phillips, M.D. director of Harvard Medical School's new Center for Primary Care suggests that more strain can be expected due to a need to absorb thirty million people. An approach most favored by experts at Harvard is *the reshaping of traditional primary care to a more efficient team practice in which patients with routine problems are seen by nurse-practitioners and physician assistants, thereby freeing the doctor to spend more time with patients that have more serious complaints.* This team approach proposes to offer medical care to more patients, but what if we do end up with a shortage of doctors within 10 years? Ignoring issues related to our present day-or even future healthcare issues-and sitting around complaining about how there is a lack of qualified physician's, or how we dislike the doctors, hospitals or governmental structure will get us nowhere. We cannot afford to continue shirking our responsibility toward our health and wellbeing as we have in the past.

It doesn't take a rocket scientist to see that all of this external stimuli has changed people. Food toxins, electromagnetic frequencies, air toxins and the like contribute to dis-ease and the dysfunction of our bodies. We need to see that we are all a part of the whole—a part of the God source that lives within each of us. We are all one. The mass and atomic structure that forms the human body are but pieces of an even bigger puzzle. We each fit nicely into the grand scheme of the universe and are hardwired into the universal cache which provides answers as we need them. We are a part of the one universal mind, the one universal body with the greatest potential.

This brings to mind an experience I had which I would like to share with you. It changed the way I looked at and interfaced with the world around me. This experience took place early in my spiritual development and awakened a fire within me that has, to this day, not been extinguished.

In my early twenties I worked for a couple of family friends doing landscaping and gardening. One particular afternoon my boss and I left the job site to go to a small park near the Delaware River in Pennsylvania to eat our lunches. We ate in silence while enjoying the beautifully serene landscape that surrounded us. I finished my lunch and perched myself up on the picnic table to contemplate my existence; wondering what I was to do with the rest of my life. After a few minutes passed I felt as if I was being lured into a deep trance like state. I remember sitting there quietly looking out over the park. The breeze playfully lifted and tossed the straggles of hair that had fallen down out of my pony tail. The trees and bushes moved in unison as the breeze moved over and through their branches. Then, suddenly, all that I was looking at broke up into tiny circular particles. They moved and floated, bouncing off one another; some being absorbed while others just moving slowly and methodically without any effort. I shook my head in disbelief and my boss, without taking her eyes off of the moving landscape, asked me if I could see what she was seeing. All I could muster was a nod of my head. It was breathtaking! As I held the intention of wanting clarity about this event, the landscape seemed to answer my thoughts. The atoms moved to show me the space that was between them— air pockets that allowed the atoms to move around without slamming into one another. They floated effortlessly in harmony. The broken landscape seemed to surround me and then quickly but painlessly began to take over my hands and then body, breaking my ego driven illusions about my existence into tiny pieces. The atoms engulfed all that I was, allowing my energy to play within its own. It showed me that I too was made of the same matter. As I watched in this trance like state, my energy danced and flowed with all of the particles of the landscape that flexed around us. Then, as quickly as it began, it stopped; leaving me peaceful, vibrating and exhilarated! A feeling of awe came over me and I remembered thinking that this experience would be the first of many to come.

Matter and you

LET US BRIEFLY discuss what is known about matter and energy, as there is a difference between the two. What I understand to be true from my basic background in Chemistry is that the Conservation Laws state that Matter has mass and Energy is the ability to do work. Matter may have energy but both are different from one another. To determine the difference you can look around at the things within your environment that have mass and whether they take up space. If something does not have mass then it is energy. Now, energy is the universal language and being such it does have a way of communicating. To those that are claivoyant, clairaudient and clairsentient, energy communicates beyond the range of the human senses. The communication can come in the form of visible light, infrared, ultraviolet, x-ray, microwaves, radio and gamma rays or other forms of energy such as heat, sound, potential energy and kinetic energy. In all cases we can simply conclude that all energy and matter can communicate by conveying images. Images are also a form of communication. Imagine for instance that you are in a foreign country and you do not speak the native language, so instead you begin to use your hands to show the locals what you are looking to find. In this instance body language can be used to share that you are hungry. Even though you are not able to communicate your wants through conversation, the locals will understand what you are trying to convey by the use of body language or images created by body movements.

When matter and energy within our environment tries to communicate with us it will do so by projecting images to us. For you to hear, smell, taste, see, or feel what is being communicated you would need to calm your own internal chatter and be in a state of acceptance so that the images being projected register within your energy field. Now, you do not always have to be consciously in a state of acceptance. When you are totally consumed by whatever it is that stresses you, energy and matter will still always try to communicate and being that time and space mean nothing to matter and energy, the message will register within our energy field to be retrieved by us when we are ready to accept it. When, for instance, you are worried about not being able to pay your bills, the energy and matter within you will act as a bumper car to all other energy outside of you. In this state it will be difficult to find solutions to your problems but if you were to breathe deeply in an effort to calm your mind and project your energy outward, connecting to energy outside of you, you will then be in a state of acceptance which will allow all other matter and energy to send you the answers to your questions. As Tracey and I sat in the park that day, I asked a question and directed it or projected that question to the energy and matter within that park environment. The questions I held firmly in my mind are, "Can the birds, wind, water, trees, stone, and soil hear me?" and "Can each respond to me?" Within seconds of asking the question the landscape in its original form fractured allowing both of us to see it.

We are truly a part of all that exists. Be mindful, when we are out of balance in our lives we tend to act like bumper cars and all other energy thwarts our efforts. When we are in balance all energy dances with our energy; for example, you may recall a day when you were driving through down a city street and you got all green lights, or an entire days worth of events went well as you focused your intention on just enjoying your day, or even a day when those around you worked with you almost effortlessly-rather than against you.

Awakening your senses

I F YOU WOULD like to try this exercise to awaken your senses, just follow these directions.

Find a comfortable place to sit, inside or out. A quiet place is preferable to noise or having other people around that can distract you. Their presence can interfere and keep you from seeing or experiencing things more deeply.

Sit comfortably focusing on your breath. You need to fill your lungs fully with air, hold for three seconds, and then exhale all the air from your lungs. Get rid of all the stale air that's trapped in the lower lobes of your lungs. This is important because we tend to be shallow breathers when we are stressed and our brains need more oxygen. Try to pay more attention to your breathing by choosing to breathe more deeply and fully each time you notice that you are breathing shallowly. After you have taken three or four deep breaths choose an object to fix your attention on. You will continue your breathing without holding your breath and keep your eyes fixed on that one object. By practicing this exercise you should be able to sense the object more deeply and as you focus on it, the structure may split apart revealing its atomic structure, much like the park had done for me. It may take some time for your inner sight to kick in, but with practice it will happen. If you tried this experiment and it worked for you the first time, it will get easier each time you put conscious effort into doing it and then one day it will happen without you being mindful. Deep breathing and focusing your awareness is the first step in transforming your reality.

How does one use the new found connectedness? Well, if you live here on planet Earth with the rest of us you know of Oprah Winfrey and her philosophy on gratitude. Moreover, showing or experiencing gratitude for what you do have, rather than these things that you don't have. This is another key to living a sacred life. Think about this;. most of us get up, eat, get ready for work or gear up to take care of the kids and never think about how great it is that we can open our eyes to see the light shinning though the window. Most of us get up each morning with a nagging voice echoing from our brain, reminding us of all the things we did wrong yesterday and all the things we must get right today. So, what would happen if you made it a point to blot out all negative thoughts with a positive affirmation to show your gratitude for your eyes, ears, fingers, feet, legs, hands, and arms? I think you get the point.

Intention

EACH MORNING UPON waking, you can speak out loud or cogitate inwardly about something you feel grateful for! I might choose to say thank you Lord for giving me another beautiful day to be of service to you, or thank you Lord for my eyes-for they are perfect, and I can now see your splendor. Keep a notebook next to your bed and if you don't care to speak your gratitude, then write it down. Be clear on your intent. I can't tell you how many people I've counseled over the years that would come seeking to find themselves, knowing they wanted *something* but not really knowing what that *something* was.

> When grandfather sun shines down on your face, know that I am with you.
> When Mother Earth springs forth new growth, know that I am with you.
> When wind spirit caresses your skin,know that I am with you.

Know that you are a part of everything that is.
In this knowing, you will be aware of your own
special connectedness and that I am always
with you.

—Nicole Myers Henderson

God provides us with many opportunities to learn.
He afforded me many as I learned how to communicate with my body over the years and I believe that you
will have many to share as you move forward. You may
recognize, as you empathize with my experiences that
your body has been trying to get your attention; trying
to bring you into awareness; into alignment with your
God-source.

I shake my head as I think of those early days. I
had my own ideas and lusted after outcomes only to
find out that some things are just supposed to be. It
took me a long time to accept that I had to grow out of
my ego based thinking; to come to the realization that
every cell in the human body works for the *whole*-every
second of the day, without our conscious effort. As we
move forward, we will focus on what I call, *Purposeful
Combined Effort*. I will be teaching you how to communicate with the cells of your body in order to create
balance, peace and joy within all aspects of your life. It
is written as a guide to get you started on the road to
communicating with your innate wisdom. It will skim
the surface of opening you to your greatest potential as
an energy being, and as you grow you will foster your
own techniques to suit your way of life. This practical
guide is a tool that anyone can use to heal from within;
to lighten the proverbial load that the body carries due

to environmental toxins, old outmoded ideas, thoughts and painful experiences. These tools can help you live in community, create peace, love, heal and can even offer you a better way of life.

I have written this in such a way that it can be applied immediately and easily digested.

By communicating with the cells within your body and tapping into your own stored memories, you will find out that your body has been trying to communicate with you since conception. It is your faithful inner guide and ever present companion. It is your loyal, devoted physician and your ultimate practical apothecary. Once you open yourself to utilizing these techniques you will come to understand that you have never been alone. Your higher self, core essence, or God-source has always been within you, guiding like a bright light atop a lighthouse, protecting you from life's rocky shoreline. It has taken care of all that needed to be done in order to keep your body alive and well throughout the years without being acknowledged consciously by you.

Most of us take our body for granted, and in doing so we have given our power away to others, perhaps wanting them to take responsibility for our health and well-being. Now is the time for us to take our power back and realign ourselves with the truth, the truth that our body has the ability to heal when we give it what it needs.

A word of warning for those that already have health issues and that require assistance from a physician: You can use this guide, but I urge you to continue your regular doctor visits and don't be afraid to tell your practitioner that you have been practicing meditation-like techniques that allow you to feel what is happening within your body and have allowed you to become more familiar with what your body needs. Some will be able to use this guide effectively while others will read it and lack the trust necessary to create lasting change. Stick with it! It will grow on you and you will be surprised at how quickly it works.

I would also like to voice an opinion. If you suspect that you have an illness that requires a physicians' attention, please do not hesitate to get the help you think you need. These techniques have worked for me and for countless others that I have worked with over twenty plus years of practice, but not all will be ready to grasp the idea that we have the ability to tap into the God-source within ourselves to heal. Not all are ready to accept that we humans are infinitely more wise and powerful than we have given ourselves credit for. Know too that this book can also be used to help you communicate what you "feel" with your family practitioner or specialists. It is my hope that you come to the realization that you do not have to leave your health and well-being up to someone that does not know you, and that you do not have to take care of yourself on your own. I used these techniques effectively during my bout with endometriosis and my physician was happy to have the additional insight and wisdom from my body. Many physicians realize the need for patients to participate in their own care and they are educating themselves on complimentary forms of medicine in order to help guide you. The tides are turning and physicians see that the old ways of practicing medicine are not fully effective by themselves.

These exercises included in the following chapters may be used broadly for business, world issues, health problems or to answer personal questions pertaining to others. As you move through them be aware and be clear on your intent as you delve deep into your God-source to watch and listen to what it has been trying to tell you all along.

Economic Awareness
and Sustainability

UNBEKNOWNST TO MANY The World Commission on Environment and Development (WCED) had 15 meetings in various cities around the world to seek first-hand experience on how humans interact with the environment. The commission involved twenty-one members that were drawn from across the globe, half represented developing nations.

In 1987, a final report was issued by the Brundtland Commission entitled *Our Common Future*. This was the first reliable and widely distributed study exploring the global impact of humans on the environment; the principal link, *Sustainable Development* being the priority. It is described as *the development that meets the needs of the present without compromising the ability of future generations to meet their own needs*. As a global imperative, it is necessary for our nations to integrate pathways associated with social equity, economic productivity and environmental quality. Each should share certain common traits which would reflect the essential needs of the world's poor, plus address any limitations imposed by the state of technology and social organizations on the environments ability to meet present and future needs.

Sustainable development is to address the social construct that seeks to improve the quality of life for the world's people; reasoning that sustainability of environmental resources and services ties together social equalities, viability, and the bearability of the human race.

Spirit moved me to begin writing this book in 2005 and it is now 2013. The Hopi Indian documentary hit the market in 1985 but led us to focus on an increase of cataclysmic earth changes around the year of 1995. What's my point? From what Spirit has told me we should be in the beginning stages of the sacred movement by the time this book becomes readily available. The reports and studies done on the issue of sustainability are of extreme importance. They are revving up our engines and getting us to focus on what *actions* are appropriate for the world's dilemmas. (You may want to take note that I did not use the word *reactions*—this will come up again in a future chapter.)

Great Spirit has given us ample time to change those things that are necessary for the human race to come into alignment with creating sustainable change. Change that will create, promote and implement programs that seek to improve the lives of the world's people.

With the availability of technology in the world today there is little reason for even one person to say that they cannot do something to help change the world for the better. For each of us to get into alignment with our own sacred time, investigation and self-exploration is essential. If you do not know how to begin, I have come up with a few suggestions.

First, *start where you are*! Pima Chondron wrote a little booklet that addresses this very concept. I love it! When I feel stuck or fixated on something I go back through the text to engage in a higher perspective. So, start with you. Use the tools provided in this book and those offered by Lance Secretan to determine what makes you tick. What are you passionate about and if you were to die tomorrow, what would you choose to scream from the rooftops today. Author Nancy S. Lawson, author of *A Final Farewell* suggested that we share the things that we would feel sad about, if we were not to get a chance to share it with the world in the future. Step two will require you to observe your immediate surroundings-taking what you know about yourself now and your need to share that with others, marrying the two. What is it that only you can do—only you are capable of—that no one else can do quite like you.

Each of us has our own special gift. Let us compare people to fingerprints. No two are alike therefore no one else can do something quite like you can. You came into this life to do something special. What is it? What does it look like? You have to always be mindful about no one else being able to do it better than you. Ask yourself—ask your inner God-self—What am I here in this lifetime to do that no one else can do as well as I can?

Step three: Follow through.

You can ask your God source about your own life force. "What do I resonate better with air, earth, fire, water?" You can get more specific by asking more direct questions that might include how your energy might work better when focusing on cells, tissue, atoms, animals, concrete, metal, vegetables, minerals, genes, germs, bacteria, the building up of, or the tearing down of something. When you are acting from a perspective of doing something for the betterment of the human race, or the generations that will come after us, you will be in alignment with your sacred time and you won't be able to stop yourself from improving the quality of life for others in the world.

Again, get focused—start with you—don't spend time fixating on the things you cannot change. Focus on the things you can once you have connected to your God source. Introspection leads to external harmony and peace. Honor who you are, take time to detoxify the old stagnant energy your body is holding on to. As we each do this we will find our outer world doing the same. As we live in the now-focusing our intention on what we can do at this time in our lives, our social, environmental and economic landscapes will change for the better as well.

We are at the crux of change. Our non-sustainable development, non-life sustaining habits create urban sprawl, impact land use and fuel consumption and we can see how these have negative health consequences for the human race.

Obesity

I N 2010, THE World Health Organization
(WHO) revealed that 1.9 billion people world-
wide are overweight, which has increased by 25
percent since 2002. We have become too sedentary,
which increases the risk of overall mortality. Our children's lives are at stake. Many sit behind closed doors
playing video games and watching television, which I
like to call the *babysitter*. Parents feel overwhelmed by
all the things they have to do in a days time and are
content that their children are just being quiet enough
for them to get some other things done.

I had moved to North Carolina from New Jersey
in 1997, and I can remember thinking two things—
judgmental as they were—about the state of the people
and the food served in local restaurants. Far too many
people were overweight, especially the children and
the restaurants during that year offered mostly fast and
southern fried food. It was difficult to find a restaurant

that served vegetables when I first got here. I thought I was going to starve. Things have changed a bit since then and we do see more restaurants that offered vegetables, but there is still an issue with obesity. Due to the financial state of many, people are gravitating to what is the cheapest thing to put in their mouths. You can't fault them for that but we can point our fingers toward those that are responsible. Us! We are not demanding better foods; we are not taking responsibility for our family's common health and welfare. It does take time to grow food, can it for non-growing season use, and dry the seeds for the next growing season. If we were only able to eat what we grew, we would eat far less and be much healthier. If all other systems in the world failed, we would have to grow our food or perish.

For those not living on their own sacred time and respecting others, they may instead choose to steal the food and belongings of others when confronted with catastrophe. You may have seen shows like, Doomsday Prep'ers where families will defend themselves and their food in times of crisis. If we truly honored each other; honored that someone chose not to be lazy and do their work to provide for their family; would we have to worry about such things? If we worked together in community to make use of the earth and its resources for the good of all; would we have to steal from others? Great Spirit is giving us time to change–time to come into alignment with this way of thinking. Now is that time.

Diabetes

D IABETES IS RUNNING rampant. The World Health Organization had predicted that diabetes deaths will double from where they were in 2005 by the year 2030. Imagine if one child alone had diabetes in your family. What would that cost your family to care for that one child? In the U.S., 10 percent of your family income will be used to care for and treat that one child due to diabetes. In the World Health Organizations region; the Western Pacific region; 16 percent of hospital expenditures are spent on those that have diabetes. In Fiji, where the country has limited access to healthcare, 20 percent of the offshore expenditures go toward treating this disease. Not only do they have to spend money on treating the disease, but they have to go offshore to do it.

The University of California offers a nutritional program through the Coursera learning platform. They suggest that somewhere around twenty-six million people have diabetes which is roughly 8.3 percent of our population, and they go on to further suggest that only 18.8 million are those that are diagnosed, leaving another seven million that have no idea that they have diabetes. This does not even take into account those individuals that are in the pre-diabetic stage. This is a huge problem because around seventy-nine million people could potentially be in this predicament.

Empty calories, lack of willpower, and poor choices add insult to injury. Even if we are financially strapped, you could still make better choices, and if you live in a place where you are stuck with whatever food is trucked into your area, you may have to step outside of your normal purchasing practices and districts to find food that is better suited for a new way of living. It will require some thought, meditation, and a bit of foot-work, but it will pay off.

Although I have addressed some negatives here in this chapter, I would like to remind you that cellular memory communication is a suitable means of evaluation for any area of your life. Including determining what your body needs in order to create balance, good health and help you maintain your optimal weight. Once you have become more familiar with it, you will be able to use the CMD method to determine what the other members of your household need.

Economic Segregation

EXPENSIVE HOUSING OR no affordable housing segregates people on a socio-economic level which generally leads to segregation by race. Not having environmentally safe recreational sites create a lack of physical activity. An increase in emissions caused by our lust for personal automobiles continues to contribute to global warming. I am guilty too, but only because we do not have available funds to purchase a green vehicle right now.

Our children emulate what we show them. If we have to have our own anything, our children will ultimately exist within that *have-to* mentality as well. An increase in roadways and parking lots needed to support our transportation system leads to water pollution and the contamination of water supplies which affects public health, increases erosion and stream siltation causes environmental damage. Our social capital or connectedness of groups built through healthy behaviors (social networking and civic engagement) fosters attitudes of trust and reciprocity, creates better behaviors, better self-health rates, and less negative results, an example of which is heart disease.

We can be our own worst enemy. Sit in on a city meeting and find out what they are trying to do to help families. Get involved! Bottom line, it's up to you to make the change for the betterment of your family and for the betterment of mankind.

Climate change

PUBLIC HEALTH IS impacted by unsustainable behavior. Climate change affects public health. Human caused activities that affect the climate resulting in climatic conditions and variability. The U.S. EPA says that changes in the Earth's climate resulted from natural causes; changes in the Earth's orbit, solar activity or volcanic eruptions. The Industrial era ushered in increasing effects on climate by adding billions of tons of heat-trapping greenhouse gases into our atmosphere that were caused by humans. Those interested in more information can visit the National Research Council on Advancing the Science of Climate Change 2010, the National Academic Press, Washington D.C.

Climate change influences heat related morbidity and mortality. Higher temperatures increase mortality rates. Urban centers are left vulnerable to "urban heat island effect" which is caused by the lack of vegetation around large asphalt and concreted areas.

Just as heat causes issues, extreme cold temperatures increase the likelihood of influenza related illnesses and deaths,pathogen survival rates influenced by climate change cause infectious disease.

Food Production

CLIMATE CHANGE INFLUENCES regional famines, causing droughts, flooding, or other extreme climate conditions having a direct influence on food crops and by also changing the ecology of plant pathogens. (Patz et al., 2005)

We are looking at food spoilage, persistent droughts, reduction in food production and nutritional quality, malnutrition, increasing fuel costs, increasing the amount of water stressed countries, rampant diarrhea, disease, poor hygiene, breakdown in sanitation, decrease in plankton, and further exploitation of the fish populations, which makes it harder for us to recover.

Increase in national disasters such as extreme storms, droughts, fires, floods, wildfires, tsunamis will result in millions of deaths.

Increased rates in Autism possibly caused by tainted or faulty vaccines further add to the vulnerability of the human race.

There is inter-connectedness between all of the Earth's systems and human health. The University of Illinois reports that public health is directly tied to the human ecosystem which humans have created by and through unsustainable activities. Human life on this planet is threatened! It's not the Earth that is at stake; it's humanity and its inhabitants.

To determine how you can initiate change, look at what you are passionate about and then ask your God source to show you how you can use this to spark change in your household, community, civic organizations and so forth.

If I look only as far as my own household, I can think of one thing that needs to change. Last week my grocery shopping cost us $214 to feed three people. Mind you, I did not purchase many, if any meats. I bought mostly vegetables, grains, and light household cleaning supplies. That sparked change in us. My husband and I decided to plant a garden. He pulled out the ole John Deere tractor and talked to some neighbors about participating in a neighborhood-like garden. I purchased $100 worth of seed and we went to work. One day's efforts will take care of four to seven families this growing season. I had saved cantaloupe, honey dew melon, acorn squash seeds, and such, which cut down on spending.

Continuing Education

FOR THOSE OF you interested in learning more about sustainability or about educating yourself further, visit www.coursera.org.

Coursera is a holding house or educational platform whereby universities offer courses for those that like learning from home. These are massive open online classrooms that allow you to take courses with others from around the world. Most courses are free but there are some that do charge a small fee. Classes are offered on sustainability through the University of Illinois as well as other colleges. These classes can help to motivate and inspire you to be who you were put here to be. This type of learning platform is an excellent way for you to dig deep within yourselves to see what makes you feel good about being who you are. The change must start with you. Dig, detoxify, adopt new life sustaining practices, and teach your children to do the same. Think about what you can create for the children to come and how you can foster life-sustaining practices that will help them transcend our old paradigm of thought.

I had originally begun this chapter by back peddling. I did not want to spend a lot of time focusing on the condition of our world. My thoughts were jaded by my own present dilemmas relating to financial security and wondering just how our politicians are going to steer this nation into recovery. But I am not so sure it is their job entirely. What I feel is that now is not a time to cogitate on how angry or dissatisfied we are at our government practices or faulty systems. To be on sacred time means, that this is not a time for separation but a time of integration. Focusing on the problems instead of the solutions can only lead to more disappointment and breakdown of organization. Separation is seen in our daily practices as we choose different business, religions, and cultural practices. We all seek to be a part of something, only to separate ourselves further from one another.

Think of the past few years of cataclysmic events, not just natural disasters, but the economic losses many have experienced. Even if you don't watch the news or listen to the radio; you may have noticed the negative events taking place in your neighborhoods, the shootings, killings, raping, and thievery. It's difficult to remain focused and positive in the wake of such crisis, death, and destruction; but I am not writing this book to dwell on those events. I am here to awaken your spirit and guide you to a space of safety and peace no matter what goes on around you-and even that cannot be guaranteed because the forces of nature cannot be squelched. It is my intention to guide you to a space where you can learn how to heal your inner and outer worlds while expanding your spiritual consciousness to create endless streams of prosperity in your life. You need to know that you have some say in how your life will play out.

The transitions, disruptions, and innovations occurring around the globe represent a quickening of sorts. Whether we are fully aware of it or not, we are all gravitating toward creating safe spaces for ourselves and guiding others to do the same. This changing world requires us to confront and defeat our inner demons so that we may be more capable of teaching the younger generations and helping those less fortunate or less aware.

If you were to focus your intention and awareness around being a conduit for such change, your God-source will lead you to be just that. Have faith and know it is done and it will be.

Cellular Communication

TWENTY-FIVE YEARS OF communicating with the human frame, animals, and the environment taught me that everything around and about us is made of energy, which virtually speaks to all other matter. You have probably heard this if you have watched or read *The Secret* by Rhonda Byrne or *What the Bleep Do We Know* by Lord of the Wind Films, LLC. I hypothesize that it is this matter that acts as a storage system of sorts that captures every millisecond of every day within the cells of our bodies. When we get overloaded or stressed these cells send out signals to tell us that they are unhappy or overloaded, thus requiring our attention in order to relieve any conflict they may be feeling. These signals may take the shape of unbridled emotions. They may appear as nervous-like twitches, shaking or some other involuntary body movement. It may feel like a pain (sharp, stabbing, chronic, radiating), a particular type of illness (Fibromyalgia, chronic fatigue syndrome, bronchitis, post-traumatic stress disorder, etc.), or it may only feel like a minor discomfort. If these feelings are merely emotional in nature rather than a physical ailment, pain, or illness, this signifies a time of ripeness within your body. It is a space in time where you can actually change the molecular structure within your body in order to bring about homeostasis—to balance the energy of your cells so that physical illness does not manifest.

Some of you may wonder how you will know if you are applying the techniques correctly. There really is no right way or wrong way to do this work. Everyone will have their own way of listening and their own way of applying what they hear from within. As you become more familiar with your body, you will know what is considered *normal* for you and what isn't. No two people will experience the same thing as they apply these techniques.

I do not want to get too far off track when talking about inner-body communication and the movement of cells outside of our bodies, but I want you to know just how extraordinary our bodies are by making statements in this and the next paragraph. Once you learn how to remedy or detoxify the inside (e.g. your inner body) you will begin to allow your inner cellular body to communicate with your exterior environment. Yes, our cellular body can communicate with other bodies, (objects, animals, and our surroundings) just as it can communicate with our conscious mind about our inner cellular body. It is this cellular body that handles every working aspect of itself in order to sustain life. When the physical body is unable to uphold and nourish the spirit, it dies. The matter and the energy within it then moves to a different level—or plane of consciousness—taking all of our life information (cellular history) with it, which can be retrieved at any point in time.

I like to use an analogy when teaching classes that may help some of you to understand. Our God-source or cellular body is much like a radio transmitter or satellite that sends and receives energy signals. When one body is sending energy out, there is yet another body that is open and ready to receive signals coming in. Those that are aware will openly receive, assimilate, and assess the information and then simultaneously respond accordingly in answer to the energy that was projected. Most unaware individuals are not able to decipher the signals coming in to them and misunderstand what they are feeling. Those individuals tend to internalize the information they pick up, believing it is their *stuff* and end up feeling quite poorly because they don't know where it came from; how or even why they picked it up in the first place. Here is a simple example.

I awoke feeling energized and ready for my day. I had my morning coffee, fed the dog, and headed out to let him do his morning business. While walking, I was rejoicing inwardly at what a spectacular day it was outside and I maintained my awareness of my feelings of deep appreciation and harmony. Along came Joe, a neighbor from down the street. I could see the sour puss on his face from a half-mile away. My stomach began to hurt. I began to rub my belly to determine what I had done wrong or how I could have caused this inner pain. As Joe approached, I crossed my arms in front of my belly unconsciously. As we met on the street, Joe began to intellectually vomit in my presence. He verbally bashed the neighbors and told me how rotten and selfish they were. He was just miserable and before I knew what hit me, my spectacular day turned into a train wreck! What went wrong in this scene? The answer to that question lies within every one of us. As energy beings we knowingly or unknowingly send and receive energy all day long. Our cellular bodies interact with all other energy no matter what that substance or material is. It can be other people, animals, cars, buildings, tables, chairs, fabric, rocks, trees, water, or even wind. We live within a matrix of unlimited possibilities; communicating verbally or energetically with all other matter in our world.

For the time being, let us focus merely on the human frame and our limitless possibilities for healing. I pulled from the internet a hypothesis which was based largely around anecdotal evidence. I have spent a number of years researching and working with cellular memory as well as feeling what others feel and I trust it to be true because of my experiences.

As described within *Wikipedia*: "*Cellular memory is the hypothesis that such things as memories, habits, interests, and tastes may somehow be stored in all the cells of human bodies, not only in the brain.*

The suggestion is based largely around anecdotal evidence of organ transplants after which the recipient was reported to have developed new habits or memories."

Posted from the same page are the reports of how cellular memory can be affected directly if the physical body is altered in any way.

An article published in 2000 in *Integrative Medicine*, a short lived alternative therapy journal, reported stories of organ recipients who *inherited* such traits as a love for classical music, a change of sexual orientation, and changes in diet and vocabulary. To date, no case where personality traits or memories have been passed from donor to recipient following an organ transplant, or has one ever been recorded in a peer reviewed medical or scientific journal.

As I read over their description, I began to ponder, *If someone were to receive a transplant and their body acted out to reject the organ, can we use cellular memory therapy to create balance so that the organ would be accepted and united with all of the other organs?*

Just as quickly as I ask the question in my mind, my own God-source answers my question with a resounding *yes*.

A few months after this information was revealed, I had my first shot at working with a heart recipient patient. What an incredible experience! The story of which is shared in its entirety in a later chapter.

I met Eric and his wife JoiLyn while participating in a health fair in my local area. Eric had received a heart from a donor a number of years before we had met, and he continued to experience extreme physical discomfort in the heart area even though his heart doctors could find no physiological reason for the pain. He was still taking a number of medications to keep the body from rejecting the donated organ and he wanted to find a way to decrease the doses so that he could live a relatively normal life. Eric and I worked together for a number of months which enabled him to create a connection between the body and the new heart. With the supervision of his physicians, Eric has been able to decrease his meds and foster trust between the heart and body which has decreased the immune systems desire to attack.

Trusting What You Hear

IT'S EASY FOR me to trust and believe the answers that come from my Source because time and time again it proves to be valid information. With time comes comfort and trust. When I receive answers, I have no reason to doubt what I hear. Those new to this concept will learn how to trust their source energy with practice.

This is a simple process. I think of a question that I require an answer to; that I could not possibly know what the answer would be otherwise, and the Source within me answers. I believe that this God-source resides within each and every cell of our bodies and it tries to communicate with us via intuition or gut feelings, pain, discomfort and even illness.

Over time, our bodies become overwrought with emotions related to past events and act out in an effort to show us that they are not capable of working at optimum capacity.

Empathy

I HAVE BEEN AN empath for as long as I can remember. The ability to feel what others feel has been quite challenging at times. It's not unusual for me to have to check in on my cellular body throughout the day in order to be more aware of whether something I feel is coming from within me or whether it is coming from someone outside of me. Empathy is more widespread then you may realize; everyone is born with the ability but one must have the desire to understand it better and possess the "want" in order to learn how to use it for the betterment of humanity. I was a very *feeling* child to begin with. I overly empathized with everything and I had a soft spot for animals. In my adolescence movies such as *The Day of the Dolphins, Old Yeller*, and *Where the Red Fern Grows* were the first to reveal the true depth of my compassion. It took many years for me to cultivate my abilities and now due to my experiences I am able to tap into this side of myself at will no matter what the situation. Those I have taught personally have experienced success within the first 10 minutes of applying the techniques. Not one that I have coached has failed to make the connection between their super conscious, God-source and body. No, this is not because I am the most wonderful coach in the world. It is because we are the most extraordinary beings alive!

Just think, if everyone were to use their God given abilities and tap into their own innate wisdom they would be more peaceful, more able to obtain answers to all of their life questions, and they would treat others with more compassion, understanding and respect. What could this mean for the generations to come? It can mean little to no mental, emotional or physical illness, less manipulation and need for controlling other people and finally, less accidents, death and killing. As I peck at the letters on my keyboard I hear my spirit humming the tune of, *what a wonderful world this can be*!

Powerlessness, insecurity, lack of control, and criticism can lead people to do horrific things to one another. When we take those things off the table and teach people to tap into their higher self they come to realize that everything that is theirs by divine right has been within them and around them all along. That there is no need to hurt or kill others, take what is not theirs, nor manipulate or control situations that could not possibly foster good clean living conditions.

Because most people are not aware of this source intelligence within them, I have purposefully done research into the field of cellular memory and formulated an easy to use technique for you to apply to your life. This I call, *Cellular Memory Detoxification*. Why? As you tap into your God-source, you will be communicating with the cells within body systems and organs; asking questions and allowing your body to answer you. As you do, your body will naturally detoxify and purge those old outmoded emotions, thoughts and events that have taken up residence in your cells. As you allow this cellular communication to take place, your body will naturally evaluate, clean out and reposition its cells harmoniously, allowing its organs and systems to regain homeostatic balance. The organs then go back to doing their jobs efficiently and effectively.

Cellular Memory Detoxification

What is cellular memory detoxification?

CELLULAR MEMORY DETOXIFI-CATION is a method or self-healing practice that I have developed over a twenty-year period, which has helped me in every area of my life. It is a way of communicating with our body systems and organs in order to assist in the freeing of **memories** connected to various emotions, past traumas and experiences. The releasing of such experiences and emotions results in homeostasis on all levels.

How cellular memory detoxification (CMD) works?

It has been my experience that the body prefers that we take a *hands-off* approach. Most often our inner-God source asks us to view and listen to what it's trying to tell us. More often than not, the body prefers that we not try to fix anything. It just wants us to see what has been carried within the cells that caused the imbalance in the first place. By giving the body our undivided attention it will bring itself back into balance with little to no effort on our part. If the body does require something from us, it will tell us exactly what it needs if we ask. Asking the right questions can be tricky.

Once you ask a question it will be necessary to assume the posture of a third party viewer and listen. Imagine hanging out with your best friend. You are having a conversation. You ask your best friend a question and (s)he answers. You do not have to dig through your memory bank seeking answers. The body will move to answer you as quickly as you ask, and it will purge emotions and memories that are stored. As you chip away at the emotions and memories that surface your body will feel lighter.

Health and Well-Being

ALTHOUGH PHYSICIANS WILL-INGLY educated themselves to help you heal your body; it's your life and your responsibility to tell them what's going on around you, what you're feeling and what you feel may be contributing to a physical imbalance. It is important that you get more familiar with your body, find out what it needs and what it is trying to tell you so that you can guide those that administer care. It is not their sole responsibility to heal you. You should willingly participate in the experience and be willing to take part in your own rescue!

CMD therapy can be used for many things. I have listed some examples for you to consider.

- Prevention of dis-ease or dysfunction
- Help you quit drinking
- Quite smoking

- Eat healthier meals
- Aid in motivating and inspiring you to exercise
- Healing from dysfunction and/or disease
- Recovering from illness such as Chronic fatigue syndrome, Fibromyalgia, chronic pain etc.
- Recovering from addiction
- Emotional and physical detoxification
- Recovering from war related illnesses such as PTSD, PCR, Chronic adjustment syndrome, anxiety
- Alcohol and drug detoxification
- Compulsive buying, hoarding and Obsessive Compulsive Disorder, Trichotillomania, etc.
- Surgical procedures
- Pre-surgical preparation
- Analysis of anesthesia
- Interviewing surgeons
- Choices in surgical styles–what will work best for you
- Post-surgical procedures
- Analysis of healthcare choices
- Choices in healing foods
- Post-surgery exercise

Your Personal Affairs

Y OU WON'T HAVE to call the psychic hotline and when you do it will be more for entertainment... you will have a direct line to the Source of all things right inside of your very own body! What can you assess with these techniques?

- Relationships – marriage
- Assessment of partners, potential partners and dating
- Trust issues & jealousy
- Work related, associations, affiliations & memberships
- Prospective strategic alliances & investors
- Future of a business
- Nature of business deals
- Family- children

- Fertility & fertility treatments
- Probability of childbearing
- Defining family size
- Impending moves
- Types & location of housing
- Religion – spirituality
- What resonates with the body
- Places to worship
- How it affects your health
- Finances – strategic alliances
- Seeking services
- Local offices – which to use
- Types of investments
- Where to put your money
- How much cash to keep on hand
- How much to deposit
- Paying off debts – how much and how often in order to maximize your resources
- Business & personal resources
- Resources you have at your disposal

Natural Disasters
and Accidents

Y OUR ENERGY BODY has the ability to forewarn you of impending danger. Your cells are connected to all other energy outside of itself, therefore, if you are tapped in and living in purposeful constant awareness, you will know what is coming and from where. Most of us tend to remain in a state of total overload due to the stimulus from our environments. Electronic equipment, weather, jobs, family, and the like bombard us on a daily basis. By remaining in awareness, you stand a better chance of positioning yourself to make it through natural disasters, and possess a greater capacity to assist others in their time of need.

While preparing myself for a trip to Tennessee to visit my father, I was putting my clothes together and chose to sit for a moment to focus my attention on my body. I questioned my organs to see if they had any warnings or wisdom for me. I held the intention of having a safe trip, up and back.

My body spoke nothing in return but showed me a filmstrip-like view of me driving along in the car. I was on a steep hill and I felt as if I was laying heavy footed on the braking system of the vehicle in order to avoid something. I sensed an obvious swerve and a sideways sliding action. I took note of what I felt and decided to just remain in a state of awareness. I was taught by a mentor that *to be forewarned meant that I was forearmed with the knowledge I need to do whatever is necessary.* I don't let things like this spook me or talk me out of going on trips. I chose to take the information and remain mindful. So, while boogying up Fancy Gap in North Carolina at seventy miles per hour, everything looked quite normal but I sensed that there was a need to slow down. I took my foot off the gas pedal and just as I did a tractor trailer driver hurriedly and carelessly veer into my lane without warning. I hit the brakes as fast as I could without losing control of the vehicle and there was that feeling I had gotten an hour and a half earlier while questioning my body. Because I chose to tap into my source before setting out for Tennessee, and for remaining ever present to the dangers of the road, I avoided what could have been a terrible accident.

Your Business Affairs

I MAGINE THAT YOU wake each morning and know how your day is going to unfold. Further imagine that you are going to encounter Joe Schmo and Suzie Q Complainer and know exactly what you can say to help them with their life so that they become an integral team member to your company. Imagine also that with this new found knowledge you can avoid potential pitfalls that could wreak havoc on your business, or better still, the economic structure of the nation in which you live.

- Investments: try before you buy. Know what and who you're investing in.

- Investors: Will they complement your strengths and weaknesses? Do they fit your company profile? Do they have what it takes to see your project through to completion?

- Employee relations: know the role of each employee. Know their strengths and weaknesses.
- Daily preparation and clean up as well as the organization of your weekly or monthly events.
- Finances and business investments
- Company debt and dissolution

Cosmetic Purposes

Skin disorders and wrinkle prevention

YES, WE EVEN have the ability to tap into a wrinkle on our face and see what emotion resides within it and what memory is connected to that emotion that caused your skin to contract and fold.

The lines on our faces and bodies are merely a road-map of expressions resulting from our life experiences.

There is no limit to the knowledge you can gain by using these techniques.

There are many ways to take advantage of your new-found wisdom. Begin your day with these techniques, use them during the day while at work or play, and end your day to clean up any unwanted energy you unknowingly carrying around with you that day that you had picked up from someone else.

Success is realized when you understand your body's inner personality and its ability to handle any situation that presents itself.

When and how to use these techniques

MORNING USAGE:
I love to start my day by checking in to see if my body needs some assistance or if it has some wisdom to share. Most often I just ask what I can do for God. Should you choose to start your day by using these techniques, you can take ten minutes to gain knowledge, refresh yourself and hear what your body wants you to know before you put your feet on the floor. This is a great time to get a head start on your day.

Your body will tell you everything you need to know regarding your organs and organ systems. It can be very specific about body parts or it can use symbols to represent what the organ or system does. For example, a pipe may be the symbol for the esophagus or the intestines, a picture of the heart can represent exactly that; the physical heart or it may be trying to draw your attention to the heart of a matter. It is important that you pay attention to anything and everything your body tells you and shows you so that you can become familiar with the way your body naturally communicates with you.

You can ask questions such as these or you can make up your own questions.

Is the body experiencing balance or imbalance today?

If so, what organs are in need of my attention?

What emotions reside within this particular organ?

What memories are connected to this particular emotion within this organ?

What road blocks might we encounter today?

Who might be in need of my assistance today?

What kind of food should I eat today to best care for my body?

What color would you (the body) prefer to wear today?

Does this body want to work out today?

What kind of workout does this body like the most?

What workout is most beneficial to this body at this time?

What will we do with our day today or what should we be doing with our day?

What would you like to meditate on today?

What would you like to talk to me about today?

Who would you like to spend time with?

Who do we need to be in connected with today? (Or you can phrase the questions using words such as, this week or this month.)

Would you like to go on a vacation? If so, where would you like to go?

What kind of house would you like to live in, the color, the type, the shape, etc…?

Where would you like to live?

Where will you function at peak performance?

What location will this body best resonate with?

What is our divine purpose while we are here within this body?

Are we in the right job situation at this time?

What material gain will we experience in this life?

Does this body want to heal?

Do I want to heal?

Asking these specific questions is imperative. Knowing whether the body wants to heal, or whether you consciously want to heal will allow you to cut through to any deeper issues that may exist. Some people do not want to get well, even if their body does. They feel as if their illness serves a purpose and they will be less apt to let go of it if they feel this way.

If your body does not want to heal, we then ask more questions which would include the one most people need to ask.

Why do I choose to hold on to this illness?

What purpose does this illness serve at this time?

Is what I am feeling coming from within me? Or… is what I am feeling coming from someone or something outside me? Are they living in close proximity to me?

This is a good question to ask when we are around other people that are marinating in nasty energy. Since we are all energy beings, we absorb the energy of those around us. If you live with, or are the caretaker for someone who has a debilitating illness you may wish to check in regularly to be sure that your body is not picking up on that person's energy. This is why I suggest that you get more familiar with your Source. This will help you to know what is coming from you and what is coming from others around you. By being aware of what is inside, we are less apt to take on the feelings of others.

What she or he is feeling and thinking?

Be clear on your intent when you choose to ask questions pertaining to others. You should never ask questions about others when you are living in expectation of them. This means that, if you *want* them to think and feel a certain way, you will most certainly end up feeling disappointed when you are faced with their truth rather than your own. When we live in expectation of others and we ask our source for answers pertaining to them, there is a chance that our source won't answer. What happens next? Our conscious mind jumps in and answers for our God-source, thereby offering information that is untrue because we are trying to control or manipulate the matter. My advice is to be very clear on *why* you want to know things about others. If you only want to know something because you are lusting after an outcome, you should refrain from asking!

> Key point number one: We must never use the information we are given to hurt, control or manipulate others. Ever! Remember: Our energy moves out into our environment like a boomerang. If you send bad energy out, ten times this negativity can return to hit you in the back of the head!

There is no limit to the knowledge you can gain once you have tapped into your own intuitive power.

You can use the list I provided for you any time of the day or you can create your own questions. The more you use the techniques the better you will get at asking questions that will yield appropriate answers. It is quite normal for you to generate your own questions once you get use to the process. As the body begins to answer you, you will learn to trust what you hear. Use your imagination and intuition, and let it guide you as you move through your body opening its virtual doors.

Anytime during your day:

If you choose to use these techniques throughout your day you can gain insight into work related situations, the people that you work with, potential investors and so forth. By asking the right questions you can avoid pitfalls, hurtles, and imposing your will on others mistakenly.

Key point number two: Please remember; if we seek to understand others and ourselves first; rather than judge, criticize and rationalize, all information will be revealed by our God-source so that we can make informed decisions (acting with life) rather than reacting to things that are happening around us (reacting to life). An example of a type of job that fosters individuals that would be more reactive to life would be law enforcement. They act with life by performing their jobs as they are taught. They wait for things to happen so that they can respond or react, in order to bring a situation back into balance. Once conditioned to a reactionary life, these officers find it difficult to act with life when they are not on duty. Using cellular memory therapy on a daily basis can help them restore and maintain balance but it might take them a little time to adjust if they have been living in reaction for most of their lives. The important part of key point number two is no judgment, no criticism, and no rationalizing what the body tells you or shows you. This is a standing rule when using CMD techniques. If your body shows you something, it is telling and show-ing you the truth of the matter. It may come in the form of images or be more symbolic-like, which means you may need to put the pieces of the puzzle together in order to understand what your body is trying to say but either way, the God-source within us does not lie. It may be creative in showing us, but it is not in the habit of giving false information. The conscious mind can be the tricky one which is why it is best to listen to the heart body, the God-source. Giving in to the conscious mind means you may end up meandering down the path to lustful destruc-tion and manipulation of others.

Evening usage:

Should you use these techniques before going to bed each night, communicating with your Source will help you clean up the experiences of the day, paving the way for peaceful sleep and a bright new outlook for the coming day. My body typically tells me what my experiences for the next day will be so that I can begin manifesting my desires while I am sleeping. Here are some sample questions pertaining to what you can learn by using these techniques before bed.

Who will be calling on me tomorrow?

How many appointments will I need to set time aside for?

Will any emergency calls come in?

Do I need to take time out of my day for myself? If so, how much time should I allot for this?

Did I feed you well today? Do you need different or specific nutrients tomorrow?

Did I do my best to take care of you today?

Do you need me to do anything different tomorrow?

What would you like to wear tomorrow?

What organs are in need of my attention at this time?

Again, you can use the list of questions I have provided for you to get started, but I urge you to use your imagination and intuition as you get more use to this process.

> Key point number three: Your body can tell you anything you need to know **if** it trusts you and feels safe with you. If you make it feel vulnerable, by disagreeing with it or being judgmental of what it has shown you, you will find it extremely difficult to get anything out of it. If it fears you or is angry with you due to past experiences, it may appear as a child or animal that has been beaten, hiding itself away inside

of your body. Or, it may show up so that you can see it but it might have its back turned to you; not responding to your questioning because it feels judged or criticized by you. You may have also explained away something it had tried to share with you.

Communicating with your Source

Tools you may wish to have on hand before you begin:

NOTEBOOK: USED ONLY for your cellular memory work – this way you can go back through your book when things happen repeatedly. You will be able to verify that you had been informed of an issue and determine whether you handled the situation properly.

Pen or pencil

Colored pens for highlighting words of importance:

(Yellow, red, green, blue or whichever you choose, this makes no difference. It is just a matter of personal preference.)

Tissues: Your body will purge without any conscious effort, so it is good to have tissues on hands so that you won't have to get up and disturb the process once you have started purging. You may sob deeply or merely cry gently, laugh, scream, kick, punch, flail your arms or legs. Try to remain in a state of compassion as your body needs to know it is safe sharing events and feelings with you.

It is also important to find a comfortable place to sit or lie down. Quiet space is a more productive space, but I have learned to use these techniques in a room filled with screaming kids and barking dogs. Once you learn how to do this you can do it anywhere and under any circumstances; during a natural disaster, a minor or even major bump up.

How to begin:

Begin by taking a full, deep breath in through your nose until the upper and lower lobes of your lungs are totally full. Hold for three seconds and then exhale out of your mouth until you have forced all of the air out of your lungs; (empty, empty, empty). Do this three more times. If you begin to feel dizzy, try using creative imagery and imagine that you are a tree anchoring your roots deep into the earth. Imagine the earth balancing and nurturing you once you have anchored in.

As you achieve balance, allow yourself to breathe normally. If you ever begin to feel as if you are losing the connection with your Source, I urge you to move back to your deep breathing.

Place your awareness on your body and your breathing. We are going to tap into your Source by asking questions.

If you are asking your body about health and body issues you can use creative visualization techniques, such as this one.

As you begin, imagine that there is a bright bar of light moving from the top of your head, through your body, highlighting organs that are interested in communicating with you today. As each organ appears to highlight itself, write it in your notebook. This will enable you to go back and review the information at a later date should this organ pop up again with a similar emotional issues.

Once you have taken note of each organ or system that was presented, *be sure to write them down in your notebook,* then go back to the first one and begin the questioning process of each organ.

> Key point number four: As each organ is presented, you may wish to begin questioning it immediately before moving the light bar to the next highlighted organ or system. There is no set rule in this instance, so do what feels right for you.

Questioning each organ:

Organ example: Brain

While still being mindful of your breathing, you will focus on the brain and ask: "What emotion resides here?"

If the brain does not answer immediately, you can use the list I have provided you with in the following pages for your Source to draw from. The conversation you and your Source will have is very much like two people speaking to one another; like you asking your best friend questions and your best friend answering you in return.

Key point number five: Trusting what is coming from your Source, (the voice), is extremely important. It is the God-source we were all given before birth into this life form. It knows all things at all times. This is true for everyone. No one person was born into this world without this same God-source energy. It connects us all and communicates to us all.

Let's just say your Source remains quiet when you enter for the first time or second time, or even the tenth time. You've asked what emotion resides here within this organ and you hear no voice. I suggest you take some time to make friends with your source. It has been carrying that body of yours for however many years you have been alive and it apparently knows what it's doing. It is use to handling the foods, drinks, and medications you have been putting into it; fixing the messes you get yourself involved in and it performs each and every task that each organ and system must perform every second of every day in order to keep you alive. It deserves your respect and you may need to apologize to it before it opens up to you and trusts you.

What you can say to the Source if it remains silent

Hello. I'd like to apologize for leaving you alone all of these years to handle these very important tasks. I am sorry for ignoring you and in truth, I had no idea that I could communicate with you in this manner. I thought I was in control of all of this. Had I known that we could communicate, I would have come to talk to you earlier. This may not be easy for me to pick up and learn, but I really would like to try. I would really like for you and I to be friends, to work together to prevent illness, heal the body, look and feel better and help each organ do its job more efficiently and effectively. I do respect and love you for all you do for me. Will you forgive me and give me a chance to make it up to you?

If your eyes are closed you may be able to see what your Source actually looks like. It may appear as your child self or appear to be a certain age that will connect you to the emotion and memory that is stored within the organ in question. It can also show up as male, female, or it may appear to be androgynous; merely taking on an appearance to act out the part relating to its emotion and memory that you are asking about.

Once you have made the connection to your God-source you should always be aware that it is within you. When you have questions about your life or if you just remember to show your God-source some courtesy (by asking it what it might want to eat during the day), this Source energy will become your best friend and inner guidance system throughout your life. It cannot be taken away from you, but it can retreat if you make it feel vulnerable, not trusted, unworthy, or ignored. It is extremely wise and can be very lazy if you allow your conscious mind to run the show all of the time. Use these exercises frequently to maintain contact with your Source. You will benefit in a grand way if you choose to incorporate these techniques into your daily living.

Key point number six: Our conscious mind is the part of each of us that knows it must take out the garbage, take care of the family, go to work, clean the house, fix the car, pay the bills, etc. It is the very controlling aspect of each of us that says, "No one else is going to do this for me so I have to do it myself." If you constantly live in your conscious mind, trying to control every aspect of your life; (striving for success, only to meet with constant barriers); you will have to be very mindful of forgetting your source energy.

You will need to make it a point to work with this innate wisdom daily until it becomes more natural to you than going to the bathroom.

After you have made friends you can go back to focusing on your breathing and communicating with the organ that you are going to speak with first.

You can then return to whatever organ you are focused on at the time, and ask, "What emotion resides here?" Your source energy answers. Again if it doesn't answer, look for clues as to why it withholds energy from you. Apologize and then focus on the list. (When you focus in on that list; while asking the question; you will be drawn to a certain word or maybe even a couple of words. Trust what you see.) Your body just needs to find a comfortable way to communicate with you and the list may help it to do this.

Next, you will ask it to show you the very first memory; (which is what I call the trigger memory); it has stored within it which is connected to that particular emotion. It sounds a bit like this: "Brain, what emotion resides here?" Brain says fear. "Okay, if this is so, show me the very first memory you have of this particular fear."

Key point number seven: You *do not* have to dig through your memory banks to retrieve the memory. If you are truly connected to your Source, it will show and tell you everything you need to know. As I stated above, before key point number five, it feels the same as when you are having a conversation with your best friend. You ask the questions and your friend answers. Just as you could not possibly know what memories are stored in your friend's body; (and you would not be able to dig them up for them); you will give your Source the same respect. Merely allowing it to show you the memory like a filmstrip, or just listening to it as it tells you what happened. It may tell you what age the memory took place, who was involved in the memory and how it all played out. You will even be able to hear conversations that your parents had while you were in your mother's womb. The possibilities of memory retrieval are unlimited.

Some people find it difficult to take in information unless it comes through the eyes. You may be very visual and need this sort of stimulation in order to grasp what the body is trying to communicate to you. If you tend to absorb information via sight rather than by using your other sensory organs, you can close your eyes and use your Inner sight to tap into the same information via creative imagery.

Tapping into your Source by using visualization techniques

Some find it easier to use visualization techniques when speaking to their body. I tend to use a symbol such as a house to represent my body.

Focus on your breathing, as I have suggested in previous paragraphs. Once you achieve the body breath balance you can imagine or visualize that you are standing on your front door step. Reach for your door knob, open it and enter. Take note of what you see as you enter. Is the house in disarray? Is it a different color? Is it decorated differently? Does this inner house look different from the house in which you physically live in presently? If so, is your body trying to tell you that it would prefer this house over the one you actually reside in? Pay attention to what you see.

Once you are inside, look for the person in charge of running the household. (I tend to look for Nikki, since she is the one that handles all of my organ and system operations. As you enter the house you can simply holler, or whisper your own name and request a response.

It sounds a bit like this: "Nikki…hello,where are you?"

She answers; "I'm upstairs in the bedroom."

So, I head upstairs to the bedroom to see what she's doing.

Take note as to how that source energy reveals itself to you, also take note of what it's doing as you enter the room. You can even ask your source what it's doing if it is not totally obvious. Have a conversation with it. Tell it how much you would enjoy the two of you working together and ask it if it wants your help. Once you two make friends you can ask your source if it's willing to talk to you about organ and system functions, business affairs or even personal issues.

You can use the rooms of your house to symbolize organs within your body. (E.g.: water in the bathtub may symbolize heavy emotions held within the bladder; a broken thermostat may be symbolic of your own inner thermometer being off kilter due to an infection or illness; the cellar may symbolize your reproductive or pelvic cavity; the attic may represent your brain, and so on.) As your Source guides you through your rooms pointing out specific trinkets, furniture or fixtures, you can ask the source exactly what organ the object represents. You can look for bumps, bruises, scratches. You can even taste and smell things or feel the texture of your organs. You will use all of your senses while working with your source. It may use whatever symbols are necessary in order to help you understand what it has been feeling and how a particular emotion affects that specific organ. You may find a few different emotions in an organ and, you may also find the same emotion residing within more than one organ. Understand that there are many forms of each emotion and there will be many memories connected to those emotions.

Let's go back to the bedroom and talk to Nikki so that you can better understand just how in depth you can get with the questioning process.

> Nikki is sitting at her desk working on some papers as I enter the bedroom. So I ask, "Nikki, what are you working on?"
>
> Nikki: "You know... we're writing a book."

Me: Yes, I know and I was trying to help our readers better understand how this cellular memory process works.

Nikki: "Oh, okay. Sorry."

Me: "No problem. So, we are writing a book?"

Nikki: "Yes."

Me: "Can I take you away from your writing to talk for a moment about our body?"

Nikki: "Sure!"

Me: "Are there any areas of the body that are in need of attention today?"

Nikki: "Always!" (She gives me a sheepish grin.)

Me: "You're so funny! Okay, so what organ wants to speak to me today?"

Nikki: "The liver."

Me: "Is this imbalance emotional or physical in nature?"

Nikki: "Emotional."

Me: "What emotion resides here?"

Nikki: "Hatred."

Me: "Interesting... I have never hated anything... hmm... Show me the very first memory you have of this emotion of hatred."

Nikki shows me a filmstrip-like memory of a dog I used to play with as a child. I was about seven or eight years old. I lived in Finesville, New Jersey along Rural Route 627. My mother always said that if you sneezed while entering Finesville you would have missed seeing the rest of it! Route 627 was the only major roadway through our little town and there were many hidden dangers if one did not pay attention to their surroundings. Cars and trucks would speed past our houses, which sat only ten feet or so from the roadway. My little dog friend was always tied by a large chain and hooked to her dog house in the neighbors back yard. Her owners never played with her and she would get lonely. I was the only one that would go sit and play with her. This one cold, snowy day she broke that big chain, ran out into the road and got hit by a car. I lived about four houses down from her and was quite in tune to her energy. I was playing with something on the floor in my house and halfheartedly watching television when I felt and heard a thump. I knew it was her. I jumped up and ran outside to find her lying in the road with blood coming out of her nose, eyes and ears. I ran out into the road, fell to my knees and held her. Her owner came out on his porch and yelled at me to get away from his dog. He went back inside and when he returned he was carrying a gun. He walked down the stairs and grabbed a hold of me, pulling me off of her. He shoved me away and shot her in the head. The emotion of hatred surged through my body again as I relived the memory. I ran to her again, pushing him out of the way. He grabbed me again as my mother came out to retrieve me. She tried to console me but I was screaming for my dog friend so loudly I could barely hear her words. She dragged me back to our neighbors' front porch. The dog, hearing the terror and anger in my voice, got up and ran to me with every ounce of energy she had left. Her owner shot her again. She managed to get to me on the porch and flopped over into my lap bleeding profusely. My protecting her only made her owner angrier. I sat on the porch kissing and holding her as he stomped over to us. He angrily yanked my hands off of his dog and shoved me aside telling me that she wouldn't live anyway. She was his dog and he couldn't afford the vet bills. My mother grabbed me and pulled me toward home. I looked back one last time to see my friend getting shot in the head two more times. She never took her eyes off of me. I felt helpless. I hated him for what he did and how he treated my friend.

Me: "Nikki, I understand the link between hatred and the memory, but why would this show up now within my liver?"

Nikki: "Yesterday you took your companion, Kiawa, to the animal shelter to be cremated. You know how much you love her and you were thinking about how cruel people can be to animals. You use to work at an animal shelter and you were aware of what you would see while you visited this one. You and your friends walked around to look at the dogs that were being held in the pens for adoption. The police officer told you that eighty dogs and cats were being euthanized per week. There were so many unwanted, mistreated animals. Seeing the dirty, frail, lonely creatures cramped into those small runs brought up the feelings you had about your dog friend being chained to her dog house. You could feel their pain and sadness. It made you feel that hatred all over again. Your liver is trying to detoxify those feelings so that you can live in a state of love. Hatred has no home in this body. It must go.

Me: "I am at a loss and feel as if I should do something. What can I do to stop the atrocities that are done to animals? And… if I can't do anything to stop it, what can I do to help my liver feel better?"

Nikki: "Tell the truth, just as you experience it."

Me: "The truth about what? I don't think I understand what you're alluding to."

Nikki: "The truth about how animals also use extrasensory perception to communicate with us. The truth about how we are all connected. We are all energy – animals included. Harmony, respect and compassion are to be our main focus from here forward."

Judging what you hear will only exacerbate a situation. Me, judging what I heard my body say sounded like this: "Oh, you're opening a can of worms. Do we really need to go there? That will have to be in book number two. I don't think we have time to go into that in this particular book. I don't mean to put you off, but if you don't mind we should really keep to the subject of teaching people how to communicate with their bodies. As I listened to my own intellectual vomit, I decided to stop myself before I made her angry. So, I took a deep breath and promised to address the subject in the next book and write about our discussion.

You see, we tend to judge what we hear, even when it comes from within, and even when we have used the techniques for a long time, but…you will catch yourself just as I did.

Instead of accepting what my source just told me, I chose to be judgmental. I chose to make up my own agenda rather than to listen and breathe. Take a look at her response to my criticism.

Nikki: "I don't think you will get to choose when it will be revealed. There are events that will take place on this planet that will align you with the proper time and place to share these truths. All you have to do is hold the intention and be who you are. I will help you when the time comes. Without judgment or criticism, I respond."

My response to her after that; "I am sorry. I know you will."

Don't beat yourself up about forgetting to stay open, just apologize and keep on going. You can have conversations just as you would with any friend. You just have to pay attention to what you see, smell, taste, hear and feel. We were given these sensory gifts for a reason. Trust your Source to guide you to the truth of a matter. Know that whatever route you choose to take in order to tap into your Source energy, really doesn't matter.

Whatever vehicle you use to "get there" will work, just as long as you get there. The key is in your awareness and intention. What do you intend to accomplish by going within? Be clear on your objective. For me, it is about maintaining homeostasis, staying balanced so that illness does not manifest, and if by chance it does, it won't stay long because I am ever present in my awareness. Do I forget? Sometimes. Will I get sick? Probably, but I am better equipped with the tools I need to get well and I am more able to determine why I allowed myself to get sick.

Let's go back over the process of communication.

Once you get inside and know that you have made contact with your source, you ask it to identify the organ or system that is in need of attention. Then you ask it to show you what emotion is connected to that organ. Once you hear what it tells you, you ask your source to show you the memory connected to that emotion. Now... you can either ask to see *the memory* or you can ask it to take you to the *very first memory* it has of ever feeling that particular emotion. There really is a difference between the two.

Key point number eight: We ask the Source to show us the very first memory (the trigger memory) it has stored within that organ in order to determine just when that emotion

was anchored. If we find the root cause or trigger memory and give it our full attention first,
all other memories will fall like dominos. The
body will then be able to achieve balance easily, effortlessly and typically, more quickly. If
you choose to start with just any ole' memory it
may take you longer to regain inner balance. Be
mindful that there are many forms of each emotion stored within our bodies. There are many
experiences that your source will want to share
with you. Speaking from personal experience, I
have found it easier to go directly to the issue
that started all the trouble in the first place. By
paying attention to that one first, all others will
just show up for viewing and not wreak havoc
on your emotional state. You should be able to
view them with very little attachment.

Emotions

IF YOU HAVE difficulty hearing what your source is trying to communicate to you, you may use this list to determine what emotion each organ or system is feeling.

You pose the question: What emotion resides here? Take note of any words that stand out or appear highlighted. I have provided a lengthy list of emotions for you to choose from. If you stare at the list while communicating with your body, your God source will place your awareness upon the emotion that does reside there. It may appear in bold print or a different color or you may just intuitively know that is the right one at that time.

1. Joy
2. Knowledge
3. Empowerment
4. Freedom

5. Love

6. Appreciation

7. Passion

8. Enthusiasm

9. Eagerness

10. Happiness

11. Expectation

12. Belief

13. Optimism

14. Hopefulness

15. Contentment

16. Boredom

17. Pessimism

18. Frustration

19. Impatience

20. Irritation

21. Overwhelm

22. Disappointment

23. Doubt

24. Worry

25. Blame

26. Discouragement

27. Loneliness

28. Anger

29. Revenge

30. Hatred

31. Rage

32. Jealousy

33. Insecurity

34. Guilt

35. Unworthiness

36. Fear

37. Grief

38. Depression

39. Despair

40. Powerlessness

Once you have determined the emotion and viewed the memory attached to whatever organ your Source says is in need of attention, you can dig deeper.

I will take a moment to go back to using the Brain and the emotion of fear to give you some ideas as to how to proceed with your own questioning.

In the following example, I give the example of my conscious mind(Me) thinking and my inner source or subconscious (Nikki) having a conversation. You

can name yours whatever you like. I use this method of documentation to keep my story telling simple.

Me: "What emotion resides here in the Brain?"

Nikki (my source): "Fear."

Me: "What is the very first memory you have of feeling this particular fear?"

The brain takes me back to the age of four. I was walking with my brother down the street, in Lambertville New Jersey, just off of York Street and Main. We lived on York Street next to a funeral parlor. As we passed the funeral parlor I spotted a puppy tethered to a vehicle. No one was there but the dog, so being the dog lover I am, I approached to pet him. The dog rushed at me and bit my hand. I saw myself scream but I felt no fear. What I did feel, was his fear of me. I saw my child-self crying and pulling away from him as his owner rushed over to grab him. My brother gave me one of those "I told you not to do it" looks and the memory subsided.

So, I ask the brain; "Is it safe for me to assume that my first experience with this particular form of fear had to do with empathically feeling fear that came from within someone or something else?"

The source energy within the Brain responds with an emphatic "Yes!"

"Can most people feel things the same way I can?"

Source responds: "Yes."

"So, how does this experience related to my life today? Or, better still, how is this memory connected to what I am feeling today as I try to write this guide to cellular memory detoxification?"

Brain: "The dog lashing out and biting you had to do with his fear of you. Fear that you might hurt him or do something to his little slice of territory, or rather what he knows to be his. How that applies to your life today is that you have to be ever present, be respectful and mindful of someone else's space and beliefs. They may have been diagnosed with an illness and truly believe that which they have been told. They do not know any other way and may have chosen to allow the illness to manifest because it serves a purpose within their life. Or… they may not believe that they have the power to heal their own body. My point is that you cannot expect that they will not defend what they believe to be their piece of real estate; that being the manifested illness, their feelings, their preconceived notions, or anything they feel unwilling to change about themselves. They may lash out at you just because they do not understand you or this process."

Me: "Source, I would think that people will not gravitate to this guide or the CMD techniques unless it is their time to shift their consciousness. I don't expect others to follow in my footsteps. I know from the experience with the dog biting me, that I was perceived by him as a threat. Due to that experience I grew up truly loving all animals more than I did humans only because humans have a choice as to how they relate to one another. Animals act on instinct just as many people do, but the animal does not, or cannot not rationalize what they are doing or how they do it. People can speak what they feel in most cases; so they should be less apt to bite or snap at someone. They have the ability to communicate their feelings if they are feeling threatened. Since I am using this conversation you and I started to help people understand how they can communicate with the source within themselves, what else would you like to share with them that might help them within the CMD process so they don't feel threatened by it?"

Source: "As it is and always will be, the God-source within each of you keeps everything running as smoothly as possible without your conscious efforts. You, the consciousness need not try to do anything in particular, nor be anyone other than who you are by nature. When you try to force things, outside of their natural order, you tend to make decisions and live reactively to your life experiences. You tend to lose perspective for what is truly important; your connection to your core essence and ultimately create situations and stories that add to your beliefs that YOU are the only one controlling your life and destiny. The God Source within each of you knows who you are, who you were born into this life to be, and even knows the roadways you can take to get there. All you have to do is trust, learn to ask the right questions and listen. You are not alone, nor do you have to make decisions on your own. Connecting with and trusting your inner voice leads to peace and harmony. Disconnection from that Source can lead to chaos, disorder, sickness and even death."

As you find your trigger memory you can continue breaking down walls by asking the source within that organ to show you any other emotions and memories that are stored there that pertain to each particular emotion. There may be more than one emotion, or there may be more than one memory connected to that one emotion.

> Key point number nine: If your body needs to release energy at any time throughout the process, I urge you to allow this to happen. Do not try to resist. By living in a state of allowance, the body can heal itself of any illness, any emotion or any issue. This is the detoxifying portion of this therapy. Your body may need to cry, to laugh, sing, cough, pass gas, excrete waste, or talk. You may hear sounds coming from within that you have never heard before. Again, I urge you to relax and allow it. If anyone is around you at the time your body decides to let loose, just smile and shrug your shoulders! By judging, criticizing, or rationalizing, what is coming out of you, you will ultimately segregate yourself from your God-source and have a tougher time when you go back in to finish the work. By allowing the release, your source will feel that it can trust you.

Imagine my surprise when one evening while sleeping my husband woke me up to inform me that my body was making noises.

"What the hell are you doing over there," he snarled, "you're making strange noises!"

"What kind of noises was I making?" I asked.

"It sounded like a thousand men were being tortured in a dungeon," he added.

"Hum, must have been something from a past life coming out now that I'm doing this cellular memory detox."

Your body will get used to having access to you quite quickly and can become very demanding of your time. Fortunately the work continues even when you are sleeping, which in some cases might be a good thing.

If you are plagued by inner gnawing's while awake try to remember that there needs to be a balance so that you can still go to work and get your job done without any interference.

I had a personal experience while I was in a business meeting with my attorney and business partner. I was sitting, listening to my partner talk to the attorney when I began to have a panic attack. I realized immediately that it was triggered by something that the attorney was feeling. I took a deep breath and told my source that I needed an hour to finish my meeting. I promised it that I would come back to listen once the meeting was over. The panic attack stopped as quickly as it started. We finished our meeting and we left the attorney's office, headed down the escalator to leave when the feelings returned. My partner watched me as I sobbed, not knowing what to say or do. I told him I was all right and that I was working on allowing my body to heal itself by using a new technique I had been working on. I told him he could go on without me and that I had promised my source that I would listen to it once the meeting was over. He stayed and sat with me in the lobby of that building in Charlotte North Carolina with people walking by watching me. No one ever stopped to check on me, which I was extremely thankful for. I was very self-conscious about what was happening but I could not stop what I was feeling. The attorney had made reference to something that made me feel as if I was not safe with him. When he said whatever it was he said, I began to wonder why I felt unsafe. This may have been a fear of his in regard to my project or his feelings about not being able to protect my patent, but as he began to tell me his thoughts, I could feel what was occurring within his body. I even wondered if he was lying to me and my body picked up on how his body reacted to his lie. It was his thought that set off a change reaction within my right kidney and adrenal gland that brought on the anxiety attack. While sitting in the lobby with my partner, talking and crying, my source showed me the first memory ever stored within the kidney that anchored those feelings of insecurity. Once I viewed the virtual filmstrip and allowed my body to detoxify itself, I cleaned myself up and went home. I was exhausted afterward, feeling as if I had run uphill for five miles without stopping. Fortunately I had my step daughter with me and I let her drive me home so that I could take a nap.

> Key point number ten: If you have to function in a work environment that is not conducive to this sort of self-exploration, remember that you can tell your Source that you need "this many" hours; (that being however many hours you need to finish up your day) to get to a safe place to do your body work. Your Source energy is childlike, in that it can get excited about now

having your attention. If there is a plethora of information your source wants or needs to show you in order for your body to begin healing, it may try to cram a lot of information into a short period of time. You need to pay attention to how you're feeling and how quickly you want to clean out your cellular body. Rest if your body calls for it.

You do not have to allow it to get out of control to the point where you feel overwhelmed. You need to know that you can be the captain of this ship and let it sail only as fast as you want it to.

Once you have dealt with one emotion within that organ you can go back in and ask, "Are there any other emotions within this organ that need to be viewed at this time?" If your source brings up another emotion you can then move to asking it to show you the very first memory it has stored. The same way you had before. You watch, listen and allow your body to purge.

You can also ask the Source within the organ if it needs you to do anything about what it has just shown you. If it wants your help it will tell you at that time. Do not think that you have to do something. Always ask the source first if it needs your help. Be respectful and it will be the same way with you. If it says yes, you can then ask it what it wants you to do. It will be very candid with you and quite descriptive. Please remember to not judge or criticize what it tells you it wants. Just trust what you hear and do your best to follow through as it suggested. I spent two weeks crying like a baby and another two weeks laughing like a crazy woman while I was working on my own life. After a month of cellular detoxifying, I felt twenty pounds lighter and had no internal chatter going on in my head.

> Key point number eleven: For those of you that suffer from delusions or hallucinations, I suggest you to use the aid of a cellular memory practitioner until you have some time under your belt with these techniques. I have had clients that were diagnosed as schizophrenic that, during the first week or two, were not sure of whom they were communicating with. They were so use to the voice inside being the bad part of themselves that they would freeze and need help moving forward. Do not fret about needing help. That's what we're here for. To find a practitioner that can help you, email me and ask for a list of practitioners in your area. Also keep in mind that most of this work can be done remotely by telephone and Skype so there is no need for your session to be in person.

There may be many emotions stored within a particular organ. Don't rush the process. Take as much time as you need. Your body will do most of the work if you apply yourself to this process. Do your breathing, ask your questions, listen carefully, view what is shown to you, document what you see, hear, taste, smell and feel as you will more than likely experience it again at some point in your life. You may get so busy with life again that you forget to connect with your Source. This is normal once your body has healed itself. We all have the ability to fall back into old patterns of awareness.

The good thing is that if you do, you will be equipped to deal with it the next time. These are techniques that can be used for the rest of your life and if you document what you had encountered in your CMD self-therapy from the beginning, you can go back and reread passages that pertain to specific organs and systems when something does arise.

Those of you that remain mindful and aware stand a better chance of not reliving a certain experience again once you have made your peace with it. Awareness is the key component in life. Awareness—being aware is congruent to acting with life thereby allowing a state of balance, harmony and well-being. Reacting to life creates distance, dysfunction, and quite possibly mental, emotional, and physical illness.

> Key point number twelve: If you are wondering if illness has manifested within you on a physical level, you can ask one further question: "Is this pain I am feeling emotional, mental, physical or spiritual in nature?" Your source will never lie to you but if your conscious mind gets involved you will hear what you expect to hear. If the pain or discomfort is truly emotional it will tell you. If it is has already manifested itself physically within an organ or system your source can tell you what you need to do to assist it in its purging and healing processes. It will also tell you whether you need to visit a doctor and will be specific about what kind. Listen and trust. There are times, as you are getting acclimated to these techniques, when you hear your body saying that an imbalance is physical in nature.

Please know that most often, physical imbalances begin as an emotional imbalance. If you find the emotion and the trigger memory that sparked the physical issue your body will find balance. If you are unsure, please contact me for a list of skilled practitioners that can assist you.

Key point number thirteen: Try not to panic if your body does suggest that the imbalance is more physical in nature. All you have to do is ask your body what it needs in order to bring balance back to that organ or system. What it tells you to do may sound silly. Don't despair, listen and be sure to ask more questions to get clear on whether your body wants you to help or not. To help may mean that you willingly eat a specific type of food or get some mild exercise.

Important: If you start hearing voices that tell you to hurt or kill someone or something, I want you to call someone for help. This is not something we encounter by using this process and we may need to dig deeper to see if some outside stimulus is causing this to happen. (This has happened in cases related to reactions to medication that had been prescribed.) Speaking from past experience, I know that hormone fluctuation and some medications can trigger thoughts such as these. So, please do not wait to find help. Be sure you have a list of the medications when you visit with your healthcare practitioner. List all medications that you are presently taking so that you get the appropriate help.

Cellular Memory Therapy for Cosmetic Purposes

HE PROCESS OF CMD for enhancing and beautifying your body is very similar to what you have just read. The main ingredient is the site of focus. Where would you like to start? I will use an example of my own personal experience to help guide you.

I chose to test my theory on a deep wrinkle or line, set vertically on my forehead between my eye brows. In Ayurvedic practices a line like this near the right eyebrow means one might have a week liver while a line near the left eyebrow suggests a weak spleen. Rather than focus on illness I choose to focused my awareness on the line itself. I did my breathing so that I could tap into it and asked, "What emotion resides here?" I even placed my finger over the line so that there was no misunderstanding about who I was trying to talk to. It probably wasn't necessary but I did it anyway. It worked and no one was there to see me do it, so it didn't matter.

I did not hear an emotion but I was immediately transported to a memory where I was watching my brothers do something and I was furrowing my brow. I asked what age I was in this memory and my source communicated that I was six years old. I heard my youthful-self thinking about how childish the boys were acting and that they should be a bit more grown up. Amazingly this line was the first one that had appeared on my face. I can remember seeing it in my early twenties wondering why it was there. After viewing a couple more memories pertaining to this particular line I came to the realization that I did not like being a child and wanted to grow up quickly. Now in my mid forty's I think about youth and wish I had played more rather than push myself to act like an adult.

You may need to work with one wrinkle more than once. I still work on that one wrinkle and to my delight it is not as pronounced as it was when I first started. I do take life seriously but I hold the intention to welcome more joyful experiences into my life.

Take your time with these techniques, speaking to every wrinkle, line, beauty mark, age spot or scar. Talk to your belly, legs and derrière. If you apply yourself to the process I believe you will be happy with the results. Your body is your oyster. The deeper you dig the more wonderful surprises it will yield.

The Body Speaks

OUR BODIES ARE trying to communicate with us constantly. It may not like something we are thinking about, something we have put into it (e.g., food, drink, or medicine) not like something we said, something we are wearing, someone we hang around with or, it may even be unhappy with our present job or life situation.

If you are not truly *tapped in* at the level described, your body may be communicating more simply by using pain, discomfort, twitches, temperatures, noises and so forth. You may wake up feeling great and begin to head out to a job you know you dislike, and "wham!" You immediately feel sick to your stomach. Most just think they have a belly ache and attribute it to something they ate, so... the normal mode of operation for most will be to go back into the house and take an over-the-counter medicine to make themselves feel better. Those of you that use CMD techniques will know better. As your body responds to your thought about not liking your job, and the stomach acts as the signal to get your attention, you will know to stop and take a moment to breathe; turning inward for a moment or two. It won't take long.

Speak directly to the pain or discomfort. Breathe and connect. Ask, "What emotion resides here?" Then ask the body part to take you to the very first memory it has of feeling that emotion. As you view it without judgment and criticism the body pain in question will rebalance itself. If you choose to ask it for more information, be sure to pay attention to what it says, and–if you make a promise to change something, be sure you are fully prepared to follow through. Trust is a two way street. When you make promises to your Source, be aware that one way or another you will be required to follow through. Your Source knows what is best for you, inside and out. You will learn to trust it and the more you respond to the information it shares, the more it will trust you.

Using a Scientific Platform for Researching the Effectiveness of Cellular Memory Detoxification Therapy

F OR THE SCIENTIFIC minded individuals that wish to seek and provide proof that cellular memory detoxification therapy works, I have broken the process down into terms that may be easier for the intellectual mind to understand. Those better with abstract thinking may like the creative visualization processes which will be revealed in depth further into the book. Either process you choose will yield results, even for those that go into it not believing. I have done sessions with others where they did not believe that they would be able to speak to their body and equally could not understand that the body could communicate back. To set the stage, I used my own first-hand experience with the scientific method that was taught to me in college. I really felt it necessary to document my cases just in case others sought proof of it efficiacy.

Since I had naturally been directed to communicate with my cells early in life, I did not fight the process but instead allowed much of it to just come to me. I began evaluating the process and formed a hypothesis. In order to prove my hypothesis, I would have to make the cellular memory detoxification method reproducible. Tracing my steps back through lessons learned via scholastic processes, I set the stage for anyone to almost effortlessly employ the CMD method themselves.

Step one: Make your observation. My observation rested upon a feeling or sensation within my body—like a pain or an ache. I chose to focus on the feeling or sensation rather than on a particular thought I was having, or an action although, as you get better at this you will be able to choose just where you will focus your energy to tap in, (E.g., feeling or sensation, thought or action), which will permit you to reside within a constant state of awareness.

Note for you the reader: If a pain reared its ugly head, I would take that as a hint that the body (cells, tissues, organs, or systems) wanted to talk to my conscious mind. Just pick the sensation you wish to focus on and write down what you feel. A testable idea will come to mind, For instance, a question from your conscious mind to the body. "What emotion resides here?"

It will enable you to keep it very simple. If your intellectual mind is quiet and you do not move toward digging through your memory banks, your bodily cells or body parts will begin to communicate. Write down everything you see, feel, hear, taste, and smell. Use all of your senses. Write down colors, time, sounds, temperatures, light levels, and so forth, until you are moved to put the pieces together. If the body wants to speak to you, it will do so without you putting any effort into it beyond the questioning process. At times clients have had to cogitate on the process and gotten answers within 24 hours rather than getting them during their first attempt. Be kind to yourself and don't fret. It will come.

Step Two: Take an open stance. Assume that no matter what the answers are that come, there is no difference between two states of consciousness. E.g.; Imagine that it is you, your conscious mind thinking a thought to, let's just say, your best friend. If you were sitting with your friend having a chat you would ask your friend a question-you would not answer for your friend. Correct? Imagine that each has their place and neither trespasses on the other. Again, you will ask your friend-the body, systems, organs or cells a question and you will obtain an answer from within. You will not be thinking that it is you talking to yourself because if you were, you would more than likely think that the process was *whoha* and opt to not move forward. So, taking an open stance means non judgment about whether you are consciously aware or not.

I will throw in another example that has to do with utilizing vitamins to assist the body in the growth process. E.g., Again, taking the open stance; we could suppose that the rate at which the human body grows is not dependent upon the amount of vitamin D it gets. Even if we think that Vitamin D affects the rate at which the body grows, which is probably not as much as the body would grow with the right combination of nutrients, it may be easier to prove or disprove that Vitamin D alone has little or no effect other than to get into the complicated details about just how much Vitamin D is needed. Keep in mind that it is far easier to examine the variables one by one rather than trying to lump all variables into one category. What I suggest is that instead of starting by talking directly to the God or spirit within, it is sometimes better to break the body down into parts. Speak to each part separately, giving full attention and merit to what comes through from each. Once this practice becomes ingrained, the body will begin to rebalance all of the parts separately and then merge, to flow energetically, unified, communicating with you as if it were only one system, rather than the many that reside within our body.

Step three: You design your own experiment. Your body will guide you. If you are too much of a thinker—always in your head—this could get complicated if you consciously put too much effort or emphasis on having differing levels of consciousness within the human form.

Note: Let me stress that the control group can only differ from any experimental group with respect to one variable; E.g.; I would not compare the heart beating in my chest to that of a heart beating within someone else's, or I would not choose to incorporate the blood flowing into the heart as it will come with its own set of emotions and memories. (There are other variables between the two groups besides that the heart is in question, such as, genes, blood type, environmental stressors, the culture one grew up in, the nutrients one chooses to ingest, etc.) Keep your experiment simple. Each person with its own set of characteristics should be treated separately, rather than broadly treating bodies based on a particular malady or dysfunction. No two dysfunctions or maladies are alike because no two people are alike. No two fingerprints, hearts or livers are alike, etc.

Step four: Test your hypothesis. Be brave and perform your experiments. Your data might take the form of yes's or no's, the type of emotion prevalent within a particular organ – or not. It is important to keep any data that "looks" bad or good. Do not throw out any data even if you do not think it is meaningful. Make notes on everything. Even if it doesn't help with one patient, it may help with another. Write down any and all observations related to your experiment that might not be related to the hypothesis. You may not have control over other variables such as temperature, vibrations – electromagnetic frequencies that are picked up by your patient that affect their body unbeknownst to them for example, the humidity in the air. Write down how the patient acts or reacts to your questions. I tend to keep a video journal so that I can go back and review my findings and make more notes.

Step five: Can you now accept or reject the hypothesis? Since we are taking the stance of whole body, whole person analysis and not lump each person into one category, it is better to apply a statistical analysis to data which will help to establish a degree of acceptance or rejection. Conclusions based on informal analysis of data may not yield the results a scientist might need to make a proper ruling. Mathematics may be useful but I am not a mathematician so I cannot say whether this method would work or not. It is up to you and you are in control of your experiment whether you are the subject you are studying or if you are studying another person.

In my case, my future experiment revolves around determining whether I can telepathically reach those with autism. How would one know whether I was able to communicate with a patient unless the family member was included in the experiment or just consulted with after, in order to confirm or deny what their child tells me or shows me during a session? Either way, I would have to be mindful about determining whether the data revealed by the child and confirmed by the parent fits my hypothesis?

Do we accept the assumption? It is important to keep in mind that accepting a hypothesis does not always guarantee its correctness. It may just mean that the results of the experiment support my postulations and that I can still duplicate the experiment but get different results the next time. An example of which is an experiment I performed with a female in her sevenites that suffered from a stroke. Her family member was very upset that she could not communicate with her mother, and I offered to try mental telepathy to determine whether I could hear her thoughts. In this instance, let me say, there were a number of undesirable variables I had to take into consideration. One was that this female spoke a few different languages when she was able to speak, but her native tongue was unfamiliar to me. Another was that the family member had an academic and more scientific background—willing to allow me some latitude to perform this experiment— but maybe not so hyped up about how her mother or family would react. When I tried to explain how I was going to forge a connection , she seemed to have a problem with explaining the process to her mother and I could feel their discomfort around the process. When I was able to connect, the mother kept trying to verbalize rather than think her words to me. I was able to get a glimpse of a "short" or "severing" within the left hemisphere of the brain. Had I felt more at peace with this experience, I would have stuck with it a bit longer to have a look around the brain in more detail which could have given the mother more time to accept me and warm up to me being there. In this experiment, I allowed my feelings for the family to interfere with what should have been a nonjudgmental investigation. I wanted to make a difference and felt as if I failed even though I intuitively knew that with time and per- haps more alone time with their mother, we could have formed the mental connection needed to determine her needs and desires.

In this instance, my hypothesis would have been rejected but there were too many variables in an uncontrolled environment. This was only one experiment, with one woman that did not speak English at all times , she had never had an empathic or telepathic experience to speak of and her family found it difficult to explain what I was doing, how I could help her, and what she could do to help facilitate the process. In order to further prove whether stroke victims or the Autistic can communicate we will need to do far more research.

Summarizing the scientific process, we begin with a question we want to answer. We move to do our background research and construct a hypothesis then attempt to test the hypothesis by doing an experiment. We analyze our data and draw a conclusion and then communicate our results—being certain to keep any and all data for future use.

Heart Transplantation and Acceptance

ORGAN TRANSPLANTATION IS an area of fervent interest to me and I am considering performing a study to determine how cellular memory detoxification can help the new organ adjust to its surroundings and make friends with the immune system in an effort to reduce healing time.

Eric Johnson was my first heart recipient cellular memory patient. His wife had mentioned that he was not feeling well, and after a few discussions about my protocol, we collectively decided to use my investigative techniques to determine what was going on and what it would take for his body to heal properly. Eric wanted to spend time around an approach that would get his organs to accept the new heart so that he could stop taking copious amounts of medications.

We met on May 5th of 2010. At the time of our first CMD session Eric was feeling achy, having pain in numerous areas of his body. He himself was rejoicing in having a new heart and he felt that his etheric heart—the cellular energy of the old heart that was physically removed—was in acceptance of this new heart and he wanted to know what it would take for the other organs and his immune system to accept it as well.

We began with enhancing his breathing and asked that question in particular. "What will it take for the organs and immune system to accept the new heart?"

His body responded with the bold statement of, "An act of God!" It took Eric by surprise.

Eric's lungs chimed in, "There is no problem here with the heart." The lungs revealed that they were concerned about the surgery experience due to feelings of exposure and terror.

Paying attention to my intuition—feeling and identifying the sensation in the lungs, I asked them to show Eric the very first memory they held in regard to terror and exposure. Eric then began to see a memory play out in his mind like a filmstrip, as if he were an outsider looking in at the filmstrip of his life. He was five years old, climbing a tree. He could see the clothes line in the yard. He swung, fell on the ground, and knocked the wind out of himself. It was a scary and traumatic experience that happened only once. The scene faded and another quickly came to his mind. This one was related to smoking. His lungs said they felt abused.

I explained to Eric that this was a good time to apologize to his lungs and ask if there is something he could do for them now.

His lungs quickly replied, "Just love me."

As if the lungs were done, the vascular system—the energy of the blood—came forward. "I need the heart and lungs to work together—in sync, or I cannot go where I need to go," it suggested.

Eric suggested that the new heart had never been formally introduced to the other organs and they were taking offense to that, so I had Eric introduce the heart, lungs, and blood to see where the conversation would go.

The new heart makes the lungs uncomfortable. There have been a number of experiences with pleurisy—inflammation of the pleura.

"What do the lungs need in order to reduce inflammation?" I asked.

Eric shared what came in answer to my question. "This heart beats to fast—in the upper eighties—no Vagus nerve attached."

"Can I slow the heartbeat by myself," Eric asked.

"Thoughts can speed it up. So if I control my breathing it will slow down," the blood relayed.

"Will the lungs accept the heart if you do deep breathing—making it more natural and more continuous?" I asked.

"Yes," Eric said, sharing what the blood replied.

What does the heart want the lungs and blood to know?

The heart said that it was trying as hard as it could. Trying to fit in, trying to get along.

"Can you cut me some slack?" asked Eric's new heart.

His lungs replied, "Oh, I guess."

I asked the next question, "What does the heart need from the blood?"

Eric responded that it wants to peacefully coexist. The blood says that it knows that the heart does not belong here, but it is beginning to get used to it.

"How long will it take for the blood to totally accept the heart so that drugs are not needed the way they are now?" I asked.

"Six months."

"What is needed for this to happen, a body communication or something other than this?" I inquired.

"It needs to not be afraid of the heart anymore," the blood responded.

"What can the heart say to help the blood with fear?" I asked.

The heart chimed in. "Can't you learn to accept my genetics?"

"I'm not programmed that way," said his blood.

"We are here to reprogram, aren't we?" asked his heart.

Eric decided to take the initiative and speak directly to the heart and the blood.

"Heart is your friend. White blood cells, I need you to love our new heart. I need you to turn off the signal that says attack, turn off that switch and turn it on for other things. Turn off the attack signal. Each time you go into the heart, turn that signal off and stand down! The heart wants it done in three months. The T cells need to relay a message to the rest of the cells. We need a truce! The heart can be stronger and happier. The lungs can relax too."

Comfortable with the progress made with the lungs and heart, we left those areas to move into the stomach.

"What emotion resides here?" I asked.

We could hear anger noises emanating from Eric's body. When this happens, we don't try to stop it. It is important that the body feels safe and un-judged. It is best to let the body detoxify as it needs to so no matter what noises come out of the body, we just let them come.

Eric relays what the stomach offers. "I have to get along with that?" it says, as it points toward the new heart. "I have to process all those nasty pills too!"

"Are you ready to release and let go of having to do this job?" I asked.

"Yeah, I guess that is up to the blood, isn't it?"

Blood says laughingly, "You're asking an awful freakin' lot dad. Adjust to less meds, and I just recently adapted to prednisone being in the body."

"Blood declared a truce! What is our need for medications? Bladder and kidneys, what do you think?" Eric resolutely discharged inwardly.

"Empty me! Rid the body of toxins, and we will do our best."

We used this time to take a bathroom break. As stilly as all of this might sound, Eric's body began to feel less tense to him with each answer the body communicated.

When we tapped back in to the body, the blood still wanted to speak. "The colon is responsible too you know!"

The colon joined the conversation. I was half removed after the transplant. The whole ascending plus half of the transverse was taken out," it said.

"What can Eric do to help the intestines feel better?" I asked. Simply framing the questions paves the way for simple answers.

Eric replied, "They say I am doing a pretty good job."

Are there any emotions there that need to be examined?

"No, I've already dealt with that."

"Do they have any advice for the other organs?"

"Sure would be nice if you all got along. The stomach is dealing with the meds okay, and I have to thank the stomach for a job well done," said Eric.

As I tapped into Eric's energy, it felt smoother, softer, and more peaceful than it had when we first started our session, but there was more the body had to say, so we forged ahead.

"Legs, femur bones in particular,"

I softly cajoled, "what emotion resides here?"

"I want to run away," said the legs.

"Show Eric the trigger memory that resides in regard to wanting to run away," I said.

"I am very young. I have this sense of fear, a very heavy fear," said Eric.

"How does this heavy fear relate to your life right now?" I asked.

"I feel financially trapped in this current position, no savings due to the use of organic foods and hospital bills.

"What is needed for the body to bring itself back into balance and allow your outer environment especially your financial condition to find symmetry?"

"Hold the vision of running for ten minutes each day. This will help to rehabilitate and rejuvenate."

"Can you do this," I asked.

"Yes, yes I can!"

"Your visualizations must include a fair amount of exertion, really see yourself, see your body exercising, legs moving, heart beating faster but normally, and see yourself doing this fairly easily.

"Eric, what do the lungs believe is needed for easy and effortless exercising of the heart to build itself up?" I asked.

"The heart says that I need to strengthen the legs and get the body where it can move faster and easier." Eric said.

I could feel Eric's energy waning. This is my final question. "How long will this process take?"

"A few months," his body offered in conclusion.

End of session.

Even though time should not be our focus when allowing the body to heal naturally, we sometimes want to know how long it will take to accomplish a task so that we can gage our progress or regression of a disorder or dysfunction. Either way, it does not matter. You just do what you feel is right for you.

It has been over a year since I saw Eric, but I called him before I submitted my manuscript to request permission to share his story and to check in. He is doing very well. He and his wife moved to Florida. He has a new job with better pay, is still using the CMD method to communicate with his body, is very happy about the results and, intends to stick with it.

Cellular Memory Therapy for Business, Finances or Relationships

THESE TECHNIQUES ARE always going to be the same. You ask questions, listen and view. The only thing that differs will be the questions that you ask. I am going to post some here for you to use so that you understand how in depth you can get with CMD therapy in regard to business and relationship issues.

Begin by focusing on the part of your body that's feeling discomfort. Ask your Source to point out the organ or system that is connected to this discomfort. If you need to use an organ chart, you can find free downloads on the internet. Then move to ask what emotion resides within that pain or discomfort. Once the emotion presents itself you can then ask the Source to show you the memory linked to that emotion. It is not necessary for you to always ask for the trigger memory in each instance although you can use your intuition, and if it feels as if you need to go that far back, trust what you feel. After you have viewed the memory linked to the pain sensations all feelings should dissipate. This is when you can get very specific about what you saw within the memory and how you can use it to shift your experiences. Be mindful of what you are shown and delve in again to have your source take you to the next memory it holds that revolves around the theme from the first memory you revisited. By burrowing in more deeply you will fine tune your skills of cellular communication and your source will begin to forewarn you about repeating old behaviors and actions.

Questions Related to Business

F OR THOSE THAT find it difficult to tap into their inner voice or source energy, the following words and questions can be used to get clearer about your life work and whether you are fulfilling your true purpose. I have also included a word list that you can use while connecting to your Source energy for specific answers regarding your questions.

My present challenge regarding work is connected to? (look at the word chart and see what word/words draw your attention)

This is a result of?

What must I focus on in order to achieve success?

If I focus on this to bring about success, what will be the secondary impact of my decision?

Is (name of the employee or manager) best suited for this (insert job skill set)?

If not, what job is this employee/manager more suited for?

What are my strengths pertaining to my chosen career path at this time?

What are my weaknesses pertaining to this job choice as this time?

What must I focus on within my business to create financial stability?

Must I further educate myself on some other aspect of business in order to succeed? If so, what should be my area of focus?

What is the best location for my company? Is my company meant to be a national, international or global organization?

Questions Related to Finances

Which should I be looking into: Debt History, Debt Levels, Duration of debt, Type of debt or New Debt?

What should I be more concerned with: Financial report discrepancies, Identity theft, Fraud, Collections, Lawsuits, Cutting deals, Communications will collection agencies?

Should I pay off all debt?

Am I an emotional purchaser, impulse buyer, bargain hunter, negotiator, or a buyer based on need?

Can I wait twenty-four hours before purchasing something?

Yes or No–If you can, you stand a far better chance of not taking on any more debt if you are able to slow down or squelch your impulse buying.

What are the best ways to reduce my level of debt at this time?

Review insurance plans and deductibles.
Use savings to pay off debts smallest to largest.
Rid self of insurances not needed.
Sell off unwanted or unnecessary items.
Dump credit cards/credit card debt.
Sell real estate/land.
Pay off college debt.
Take the bus to work or purchase car with cash from what you save each month from savings
Take on a part time job after full time hours so that you don't have time to go shopping for things you don't need

or volunteer to help others in need if you do not need the extra money but want to refrain from spending.

What types of savings or investments are the smartest for me at this time?

Annuities
Health savings
Bonds: Savings / government
Single stocks
Money markets
CD
Mutual Funds
IRA / Roth IRA/ tax free or pre-taxed retirement plan
401 k / Roth 401 k
403 b /or 457 plans
Federal Thrift Savings
Gold, Silver, other metals or minerals
Real Estate / rental real estate
Long term investments
Short term investments
Risky investments
Liquid investments
Simplified Employee Pension Plan (SEP)
Education Savings

Word chart

I have put them into categories to help you understand just what part of your business or finances may be affecting your inner balance. It is not necessary that you use this word chart if you have connected to your source but if you do use this list, you may want to add others to it as you go—Do what feels right for you.

Accounts payable(s)
Accounts Receivable(s)
Assets
Buy
Commitment
Communication
Control
Debits
Debt
Accuracy
Effectiveness
Efficiency
Expansion
Expenses / cost
Lease
Loan

Local
Location
Manage/management
New
Organization
Outdated
Own/ownership
Relocation
Rent
Revenue
Sales

Scheduling
Sell
Stewardship
Time
Upgrade
Used

Assistance
Advertising
Budgeting
Burnout
Communication
Consultation
Cultural
Development
Downsizing
Dump debt
Extra job
Focus
Follow up
Global
Invest
Language(s)
Multi-cultural
Nationwide
Goals
Planning
Profit(s)
Quality / quality control
Regions
Research

Saving
Useful

Delegation
Delusion
Dishonesty
Grounding
Honesty
Direct relationships
Indirect relationships
Internal conflict
Loss
Manipulation
Meditation / prayer
Morality
Personal conflict
Personnel Problems
Religion (company politics)

Relationship compatibility

WOULDN'T IT BE a great idea if we took time to determine just how compatible we are with someone before we leap into a relationship? CMD therapy can help you find out whether you are headed for trouble or if you have chosen the ideal mate. If you know what you're getting into from the start you will choose to love your mate for who they are, rather than expending your valuable energy trying to turn them into someone or something you think they should be.

My relationship with _____ (insert name) _____ is mainly functioning in what manner?

Physical
Mental
Emotional
Spiritual

I am compatible with ____(insert name)____ in what way(s)?

Trust
Honesty
Faithfulness
Changeable
Controlling
Manipulative
Support (supportive)
Financial support
Friend
Family
Children
Karmic Debt
Opposites
Father image
Mother image
Possessiveness
Stagnation
Strife
Life/body vibration
Financial attraction
Attraction
Sexual attraction
Mate potential
Unconditional love
Conditional love
Master vibration/ past life teachings

Does ___ (insert name) ____ complement my strengths and weaknesses?

Yes
No
How?

(Insert name) _____ is compatible with me in what way?

Physically
Mentally
Emotionally
Spiritually

This person is compatible with me on what level?

Trust
Honesty
Faithfulness
Changeable
Controlling
Manipulative
Support (supportive)
Financial support
Friend
Family
Children
Karmic Debt
Opposites
Father image

Mother image
Possessiveness
Stagnation
Strife
Life/body vibration
Financial attraction
Attraction
Sexual attraction
Mate potential
Unconditional love
Conditional love
Master vibration/ past life teachings
Guide
Negative influence
Positive influenceLiberator
Guard/ ProtectorJester/ Entertainer

Is it for my highest and greatest good to stay in this relationship?

Yes
No

What do I stand to gain if I stay within this relationship? If I leave this relationship?

The main issue(s) in this relationship involve(s) what?

Trust
Honesty
Faithfulness

Changeable
Controlling
Manipulative
Support (supportive)
Financial support
Friend
Family
Children
Karmic Debt
Opposites
Father image
Mother image
Possessiveness
Stagnation
Strife
Life/body vibration
Financial attraction
Attraction
Sexual attraction
Mate potential
Unconditional love
Conditional love
Master vibration/ past life teachings

What is the potential of this relationship lasting?

Short amount of time
Mediocre
A long time

As long as you are truly tapped into your source energy you will receive truthful answers. Be aware of whether you are digging too deeply, lusting after outcomes or if you are merely asking questions and receiving answers effortlessly; as if having a conversation with your best friend. As soon as you lose track of the God-source or you can no longer hear its answers, you need to stop, go back to the beginning and start over.

Key point number fourteen: You can use CMD therapy to speak to your source about anyone or anything. (Animals, people, objects, places or other – there is no limit to what you can get answers to.) There is another name for this sort of excavation of information; it is called Remote Viewing. For more information on these techniques and practical applications please visit: www. remoteviewers.com

The Western Institute for Remote Viewing was founded by Dr. Wayne Carr. He has a team of experts available to aid you in your personal and business affairs should you feel inclined to utilize their services.
The following pages are included so that you can understand what your Source energy is trying to communicate to you. Be mindful of connecting to your God-source first before you look at these charts. As you ask your questions, source will lead you to the correct word (organ or organ system).

Systems of the body

Question to ask: What system is in need of attention at this time?

Other questions to ask: The origin of the present condition involves which system?

Integumentary: Skin
Skeletal
Muscular
Nervous
Endocrine
Cardiovascular
Lymphatic/Immune
Respiratory
Digestive
Urinary
Reproductive

Other words the body may use:

Cells
Tissues
Para-sympathetic
Chakra
Sensory
Genital
Sympathetic
Psychological
Circulatory
Spinal
Glandular (Endocrine) System
Pineal
Pituitary
Mammary
Thyroid
Parathyroid
Parotid
Thymus
Spleen
Lymph
Pancreas
Adrenal
Ovaries
Prostate
Testes
Liver
Pancreas

One or more of these may also reside within the digestive system, but I will place them here for simplicity sake.

Condition

Question you can ask: This dysfunction is manifesting as what sort of condition?

- High
- Normal
- Low
- Acute
- Aching
- Chronic
- Sudden
- Constant
- Under-active
- Over-active
- Intermittent
- Insufficient
- Sufficient
- Deficient
- Excess/ excessive

Is it necessary that I assist in the healing?

Yes
No

(Wait for your source to answer – when it does, you can move to ask the next question.)

What can I do to help you?
Nothing or something else-please elaborate
_____.

Source of the present condition

Question you can ask: What is the source of my present condition?

- Diet
- Beliefs
- Past
- Karma
- Emotions
- Nutrition
- Toxins- internal
- Heavy metals
- Other
- Toxins – external

- Land
- Air
- Water
- Electromagnetic frequencies
- Other

Chakra imbalance
Suppression / blockages
Constitution/will (extreme or lack of)
Color/ light deficiency
Influence by others
Allergic Reaction
Imprint (other)
Imprint (mother)
Imprint (father)
Family lineage
Spiritual interference/ influence
Unresolved spiritual issues
Unresolved emotional issues
Unresolved mental issues
Unresolved physical issues
Unconscious thoughts
Traumatic experience(s)
Surgery/ medical procedure
Childhood medicine/ inoculations
Bacteria/ virus invasion
Genetic inheritance
Adult medicine
Fungus
Parasites

Prior injuries

What, if anything, can I do to help you? (Wait for your Source to answer.)

Nothing or _____.

What type of diet or lifestyle change is needed at this time?

- Mediterranean
- Atkins-high-protein, high-fat, low-carbohy-drate diet
- Vegan-no animal products
- Vegetarian-eat vegetables, fruits, grains, seeds, usually eggs, but no meat or fish
- Other

Origin of the dysfunction

Question to ask: The dysfunction is located in which part or parts of my body?

Other question you can ask: What other body parts require my attention at this time?

- Mind
- Head
- Sinus/ Nose
- Mouth/Tongue
- Teeth
- Ears
- Throat
- Eyes

- Abdomen
- Stomach
- Rectum
- Liver
- Spleen
- Pancreas
- Kidney
- Bladder
- Larynx
- Trachea
- Back/Spine
- Heart
- Upper limb
- Lower limb
- Reproductive organ(s)
- Lungs/Bronchial
- Skin
- Nerves
- Shoulders
- Neck
- Tissue
- Gland(s)

Final Review of the CMD Method

B Y NOW YOU have figured out that you can use CMD methods to go within, communicate with your God-source and retrieve wisdom regarding any question you have about your life. It's time to go back and review the CMD process.

1. Choose a quiet place to do your inner work. Peace and quiet are essential when you are trying to hear what your body is saying. (It is not necessary for you to spend a lot of time doing this once you have made contact with your cellular body, but it can be beneficial if you practice these techniques daily until you have reached a constant state of awareness. When you get to this point you will have attained a state of serenity and awareness that no one can take away from you, nor be able to penetrate with negativity.)

2. Breathing is very important. Your body and brain need this in order to function at a deeper, more connected level. If you lose track of your source, breathe deeply and you will be able to reconnect.

3. Choose the route that you will take when communicating with your cells. You can use one that I have suggested below or find your own way of communicating with your body. There is no wrong way to do this. It will just depend on what you are consciously willing to allow and how your cellular body chooses to participate.

A. focus on a particular pain to speak directly to it

B. focus on a particular health ailment and speak directly to the weakness that resides within you

C. Focus on a particular organ that you know you are having physical issues with

D. Focus on your breathing and use visualization techniques. E.g. Imagine or visualize that you are entering a house, entering and finding your inner child or spirit, in order to begin the questioning process.

E. Focus on a particular business project

F. Focus on a particular person

G. Focus in a particular issue

H. Focus on a particular animal

I. Focus on a particular structure

4. Once you have chosen how you will communicate with your source, and what topic or concern you will be focusing on, you will reinitiate your deep breathing. Try to relax.

5. Once you have established contact and you begin hearing that small voice from within you can start the questioning process. Remember to be clear on your intent.

What do you want to accomplish by speaking to your cells?

Do you want to heal your physical body or a particular malady?

Do you want to clean out your emotional body in order to relieve tension and prevent illness?

Work on a career change?

Find out what your inner spirit knows you should be doing with your life?

Find resolution in relationships with relatives, family or co-workers?

Get information about a business partner or potential investor?

Gain information about a vehicle, house, animal, object, or something other than these listed?

Communicate with a loved one that has passed on?

(Energy never dies even after the physical body leaves this plane of consciousness. Yes, you can tap into the energy of a loved one that has passed away.)

The questions you can ask are unlimited. All you need to do is be sure you know what information you are seeking in order to gain clarity about a situation.

6. Begin your questioning. If your questioning is health related you can begin with this:

What emotion resides here?

If your questions relate to something other than health you can begin with whatever is on your mind. E.g., Business: What emotion resides within my body regarding my present job or career path?

You can get much deeper into the questioning than this. Just be open-minded and be sure to write your questions down so that you can write the answer your body gives you. By doing so, you will be able to go back and reread your entries in the future which will also help to keep you on track and show you how you may be repeating certain lessons in your life.

7. Once you find the emotion, ask your body to show you the trigger memory related to this emotion. (Trigger memories may take you back to a past life event, can go back to you as a fetus in your mother's womb, or it can take you to any part of your life where your perception of an experience created an adverse reaction. Stay open and non-judgmental about what you see.

8. Once your source shows you the past memory associated with the emotion, you can then ask your body to tell you how that past memory is connected to where you are in your life right now.

9. Always keep in mind that you can ask questions about anything you like, but try not to lust after a particular outcome. When you are pushing your body to give you information about something that is not "yours by divine right" you may not get the answers you truly need.

Trust what you hear your God-source telling you. If you do, you will have tapped into a wealth of information that will aid you in every aspect of your life. Your journey has just begun. Please understand that my way is not the only way. There are many great books, products and services on the market these days that are just as easy to incorporate into your daily living. Cellular Memory therapy is a piece of the puzzle that will change your life and transform the way you care for yourself and others. It is a way to treat your body, mind and spirit to a total overhaul without the need for medication, doctors and over the counter products.

If you are presently on medications, I would not suggest that you go off course by stopping them without discussing it with you healthcare provider. You can however incorporate the CMD techniques into your life, communicate with your God-source and find out what it wants and needs so that you can meet with your healthcare practitioners to discuss what you have come to understand about your body. Just as we should not self-medicate (without knowing and understanding what, why, or how), we should also not eliminate medications without a more in depth discussion with healthcare providers—in some instances there is a tapering off period that is necessary. With this I will also say that if you have been physically sick for some time or you have experienced symptoms of illness but have not seen a health care professional, it is always best to have your physician walk with you through any new process. It is important that they know what you are using and how it is working for you. Choose to live your life purposefully and in a state awareness! You will be happier and healthier if you do.

World healthcare *is* changing, so why not shift our focus to altering our perceptions of who is in charge of healing our bodies. Concentrate on erasing old beliefs or bad habits and support a new model of healthcare. Eat nutritiously, exercise, meditate, communicate with and be kind to your body. Act responsibly-take charge of your own well-being and collaborate with your healthcare practitioners. Do things you love to do and avoid those things that sap your energy!

How to use your newfound abilities

WHAT CAN ONE do with a more pronounced connection to intuition? My answer is quite simple—Anything you want! I would however, like to advocate that you willfully choose not to hurt others, trespass on their thoughts or use private information to ruin their lives.

Here are some examples of what I have used my abilities for over the past twenty-five years.

Motorsports

In 1994, my father invited me to a NASCAR Winston Cup race in Richmond Virginia. I remember telling him that I wasn't interested in watching a bunch of grown men chase each other around in a circle for three hours or more. I didn't understand his passion for it until my first race. I took a friend with me and we spent the weekend meeting Dick Trickle, Jimmy Hensley, Rusty Wallace, Sterling Marlin, Dale Earnhardt and many others. It did not take long—I think we had been there a couple of hours and I got caught up in what the team members were feeling. To say that I was caught up, is putting it mildly. I fell head over heels in love with the dynamic energy.

My father's invitation put us smack dab in the middle of the garage area where all the action was. We were up close and personal with the blood, sweat and tears that the team members put into performing each weekend; the car fabricator, engine builders, mechanics, crew chiefs, managers, gas men, tire guys, painters, pit crew and so forth. Everything they are and experience in their own lives goes into the energy of their cars. Essentially, that car becomes a living mass of energy due in part to the input of each person that works on it. So, what happens when one team member is experiencing problems in his or her personal life? You probably guessed–all that negative energy affects the car and the rest of the race team; and in racing, even the slightest issue can create big problems.

1997 Dover Delaware. I was at the track doing research and development on a simulator system that I was gearing up to build. My idea was in the patent pending stage and many of the teams had gotten to know me because of my research but some knew that I was able to see into the cars and feel potential problems before they happened.

Saturday around 4pm I was wrapping up my day when a crew chief from one of the teams approached me. He said that he had heard through the grapevine that I was able to see into racecars and determine whether any mechanical issues exist or if there are any problems between the car and driver. They were under time constraints and they wondered if I could go to the garage, put my hands on the car, and tell them if any issues exist that they can get control of before Sunday's big race.

I told him that I could help him but that I did not have to go see the car. I closed my eyes briefly and told him that I could see them standing with the car on Sunday morning; there would be a puddle of oil under the front end. The feeling I got from the engine was a lot like what I feel when I sense the regurgitation of a heart valve in a patient, which led me to conclude that this was in fact an engine problem.

He shook his head in disbelief and took me by the arm, leading me into the garage. He insisted that I touch it. I stood before the car with him by my side. No one else was there with us, which suited me; I did not want to have to explain what I was doing. I closed my eyes and put my hand on the car, took a deep breath, moving my energy over and through the powerful beast. When I opened my eyes, we were no longer alone. The team had huddled around protectively guarding us. This industry was so competitive.

I shook my head and reiterated that Sunday morning they would find that the car puked up oil, but not before then.

The crew chief was ticked off. They had just changed the engine and he did not want to believe what I had just told him.

I shrugged my shoulders and reminded him that he asked me for help, and that what I shared with them is what the car revealed. I was only the messenger. I picked up my briefcase, watched them cover the racecar and headed to my own vehicle to return to the hotel.

Sunday morning came quicker than I wanted. I was so tired that I had forgotten about my chat with the team about their car on Saturday. All the weekend traveling and grueling research was wearing me down. I grabbed a quick bite of fruit and headed back to the track to do it all over again.

It was a beautiful morning but I could feel static in the air. I tend to feel this more so when someone is thinking of me, so I readied myself for a confrontation, still forgetting about the afternoon before.

I had gotten ten feet through the garage gate when all of a sudden I felt hands on my arms and back. I was being pulled through the garage by three members of the team that I had spoken with the night before. They were excited and laughing but would say nothing, putting my energy on high alert. They pulled me toward their racecar; low and behold, there it was; a puddle of oil under the front end. With a befuddled look on my face, I shrugged my shoulders as if to say, what….you want me to say I told you so!

The crew chief took me by the hand and towed me toward the team hauler where the owner sat waiting on me. As we entered the back of the car carrier everyone was looking at me. I felt like a kid being taken to the principal's office in grade school after doing something wrong. We marched past the pit crew that was readying themselves for the big race and went through the door to the back office where the owner and team manager were waiting. The owner was not laughing. He looked up over his glasses, poker-faced, and said, "Impressive. Can you do that with people too?"

"All day, every day," I replied.

He smiled – "You're hired! Come to the shop Monday morning and we will talk it over."

Healthcare Problem Solving

I WAS VISITING MY Attorney, Michael Burgner to square away paperwork for my staffing business. I inquired about his family because I knew that his son, Kaden was experiencing health issues that had been related to his birth. He told me that Kaden was still vomiting blood repeatedly and they had gone through countless sheets, pillows and a number of mattresses due to this unresolved issue. Kaden had been born with the umbilical cord wrapped around his neck and a medical procedure had to be performed to repair the damage. Since that time, he vomited blood and his medications were providing little, to no relief. He and his wife Erin were beside themselves, fearing that they would not be able to get this issue under control. Constant doctor's appointments and medication—they were feeling defeated and in dire need of a solution. Feeling their frustration, I offered my assistance. If he and his wife were interested, I could pop by and place my hands on their son on Sunday morning to see if his body would show me where the problem was located. I suggested it might take ten minutes or so but that should be enough time for me to see if Kaden's body would reveal the source of his dysfunction.

He agreed.

Sunday morning, I pulled into his driveway and was greeted by Michael and his two beautiful Husky's. We exchanged the usual niceties and moved into the house where his wife, two children, mother and father were seated. He introduced me to everyone and then brought his son out to meet me. His mother and father left so that we could focus on the issue at hand and I suggested that Kaden sit on his father's lap in order to make him feel more comfortable. I first took a moment to assess Kaden's appearance. He looked pale and very frail. I sat down on the seat next to them and told them that I was not going to do anything to hurt him. All I needed to do is place one hand on his chest and one on his back, close my eyes and see whatever his body wanted to show me. He shied away from me at first but his father pulled him closer to make him feel more comfortable.

I breathed deeply and waited patiently until I could see Kaden's face in my mind's eye. It wasn't long before his face appeared before me and his energy welcomed me in. Seconds passed, his energy settled nicely allowing me to take a look around at other organs and systems. I felt his inquisitive nature open to me and I chose this time to pose a question to see if his body would guide me to the location that was causing the disturbance. The body responded to my query and I found myself being transported to the thoracic cavity–positioning me right on top of Kaden's diaphragm. I looked down to assess all that lie below me but my attention was pulled back upward instead. What appeared before me was tunnel-like, tissue textured, with a vast network of veins intertwined throughout. The veins then faded into the background and I was then peering at the tissue of the esophagus. I felt as if I was waiting for something-unable to divert my attention to any other area as his body-the esophageal tissue held my attention. Seconds passed. Then, six or seven inches above me a balloon began to form. One vein reappeared and began to back up and fill with blood. When the balloon could expand no more, a fissure or crevice appeared in the esophageal wall and the blood came pouring out, right past me and into the gut. I felt the nausea building, and when Kaden's little stomach could take no more, I could feel the projectile force of the blood moving up and out of his body. The dense liquid that was not expelled upward moved through the small, then large intestines and out through the rectum.

I explained what I was seeing and asked for permission to share my findings with a friend in the healthcare industry that would be able to help me put the information into words their physicians would understand.

They approved and I departed.

I stopped by my friend Becky's place to see if I could borrow her medical journals and have her collaborate on this case. I love including her in my research. When I describe exactly what I am seeing, she is able to put the pieces of the puzzle together and tell me precisely what the organ or system is supposed to be doing. We found the specific section in the medical journal to confirm that I was in fact looking at the esophageal tissue and the network of veins that I had seen while laying hands on Kaden. We took all of my information, put it to paper-in medical terms that their physician would understand and could relate to. I set up a dinner at my place and invited everyone over to review the material Becky and I had put together.

Let me say, in a situation such as this, it is only natural for people to be a bit skeptical, so I do not fault anyone for feeling this way. I learned a long time ago that in order to make others feel more comfortable about what I was able to do, I made it my job to educate myself more fully on many different subjects. By providing in-depth information to the family, I am able to lighten their emotional and mental load, making it easier for them to try on the holistic approach, since the normal investigative methods were not working. This made the

Burgner's feel more confident and comfortable about explaining to their health care provider that they saw a holistic health consultant, or as Michael sometimes describes me, a spiritualist.

Michael and Erin met with Kaden's doctor whose traditional background was in natural medicine. Michael laughed while telling me that he explained to her that they saw a spiritualist and asked her if she was bothered by it. She reassured them that she was quite comfortable with it because she was from India, and they too would have utilized something similar there- she was not judgmental at all. After reviewing the information they made the decision to take Kaden off all of his medication to see if that would make a difference.

I spoke with Michael recently and he disclosed that Kaden vomited once the week following that last doctors visit after stopping his meds, but that he has had no such event since that time. He is tall, eating foods most kids love to eat, sometimes suffers from heartburn or reflux, but he has grown exponentially and is a normal teenager.

Assisting Animals:
The Show Calf

J OHN AUSTIN, A friend of ours called my
husband one spring morning and asked him if he
could help him and his father load a one thousand

plus pound calf into a trailer to transport it to NC State Veterinary College. They had been cutting off the young gal's horns to ready her for a show when she got upset and turned herself upside down in the headstall. She was all right but not moving and they feared she had hurt herself badly. Not wanting to take any chances, they decided that getting her into a trailer with the help of friends instead of putting her on her feet would be the best way to help her.

After Monty hung up the phone he explained what John had told him. My love for animals led me to invite myself along to see if I could help. It was a nice drive through the countryside to Marshville and it gave me time to check in with Spirit to see if I could find out how this would play out. Spirit assured me that she would load well but the end result might not be as positive. I tried to remain optimistic and inwardly focused on having a better outcome than what Spirit anticipated. An hour later we pulled into the farm driveway to meet John, his father and farm hand.

As we got out of our truck we noticed that the headstall had been disassembled and the calf lay in the field peacefully, seemingly unaffected. As we approached her she shifted her weight but she did not try to move her legs at all.

I stood by impatiently, while the guys put together the equipment and tools they needed to get her into the trailer. Not able to wait any longer, I asked for permission to walk into the field to greet her while they did what they had to do. John's dad forewarned that cows tend to thrash when they're hurt like this and he asked me to use great care in approaching her. I agreed and climbed the gate to get a closer look.

She watched me intently as I approached. When I was about a foot from her I knelt down, outstretched my hand and began to breathe deeply and slowly in order to slow my heartbeat. She sensed the calmness within me and settled, allowing me to stroke her head and back. I spoke telepathically to her and explained what they were about to do to help her. As I carefully surveyed her energy I asked her if she wanted to tell us what part of her body had been affected by the fall.

Her eyes opened wide when she heard my thoughts and she perked up, acting interested. I positioned myself right up against her back. I was far closer than the owner was comfortable with, but I assured him that she would not hurt me. I closed my eyes and breathed deeply again. Her voice was soft and peaceful-greeting my energy as I entered her body. She guided me to view her spine. As I followed the energy of her spinal cord, I noticed there was a break in the nerve conduction to certain organs and also to her hind legs. The legs felt heavy and immovable. Now, the farm hand was coming with the backhoe, and John was positioning the truck and trailer. Their idea was to move her onto a pallet and then use the backhoe to lift the pallet into the trailer to take her to Raleigh.

I hugged her and telepathically told her exactly what she could expect from all of the commotion and asked her to be real still. I told her that we would have to flip her over onto her other side once we got the pallet positioned under her. She promised that she would trust me to do what was necessary. The guys were frantic about me being so close but I assured them that she promised to stay still while we turned her over. They were amazed that she allowed us to manhandle her without thrashing around. Within ten minutes we had her on the pallet, transferred both to the trailer, got everything tied down and off they went to the Veterinary College.

A day or so later I called to check on her, asking if a visit was allowed. He said that the Veterinary College was using hydrotherapy on her and that it was working. She was up, walking and eating, and it looked promising. She had a fracture around the lumbar area and it would be a toss-up as to whether she could be rehabilitated due to her size and weight but everything was going better than they had expected. They would allow us to come by for a visit.

The care team had just finished putting her in her stall after a swim in the hydrotherapy tank when we arrived. She was standing up eating as I climbed through the stall gate. She greeted me as if I were an old friend and nuzzled my hands affectionately. I kissed and hugged on her while my husband stood outside taking pictures. I laid my hands on her and her lovely peaceful voice filled my head. She thanked me for coming and said that she was not sure that their efforts would be rewarded. She did feel better now that she could stand and she especially enjoyed the water pool therapy. We gave her some extra love, said good-bye and she settled in to lie down for a rest.

One week later I was awakened from a dream state with tear drenched cheeks. Her tender loving voice lingered in my head. The dream was so real. I felt as if I was right there in her stall with her, smelling the urine drenched hay. She informed me that she had fallen during the night and reinjured herself. She knew her owner would choose to put her down and she wanted to say goodbye. She peacefully thanked me for being her friend and drifted off.

I got out of bed and called her owner to see how she was doing. He informed me of her late night fall and said that he had no choice but to put her out of her misery. An animal that size would take more money and time to heal than he had to spare, which he was clearly not happy about.

I shared his sadness and communicated my dream to him, being certain to tell him that she was aware of how much he loved her. She loved that about him—he had such a tender heart.

Parkinson's Disease

P ARKINSON'S DISEASE IS an incurable progressive nervous disorder that is marked by distinct symptoms; examples of which would be, trembling hands, shaking head, lifeless face, monotone voice and a slow shuffling gait. It is a debilitating disorder that also has the propensity to rob one of the ability to speak. Such was the case with Carol Bondy's father. He was a tall and robust man in his early days but now he has difficulty walking, feeding himself, and performing routine tasks that most of us take for granted.

Carol and I were talking one afternoon by phone and she was relaying her frustration about the level of care George was getting. He now had limited ability to convey his needs verbally and on top of his Parkinson's he also had diabetes which was not being addressed the way she felt was necessary. She was exhausted from trying to figure out what to do to help him and Spirit had informed me that she was expending too much energy on the negative issues. Her father has always been such a vibrant man, and seeing him this way really upset her. As she conveyed the mishaps they were experiencing with the care team, she mentioned that she would really like to know exactly what he was feeling about the whole thing. She had been to the facility to meet with the team on numerous occasions to talk to them about the setbacks but her repeated requests for change fell on deaf ears.

Feeling her sadness, I compassionately offered my services and suggested that we go talk to George. She thanked me for wanting to help but reiterated that he really was not able to speak at length and felt that this might not be the best approach. Without pushing, I gently reminded her that I was a telepath and he would not have to speak per se. She could ask questions, which I might revise in order to get to the heart of any issue, and then he could answer via mental telepathy so that I could translate his answers out loud to her. She seemed a bit skeptical and unsure but felt that she had no other immediate solutions so she would allow me to try. We agreed to meet at the assisted living facility over the weekend so that I could steer clear of Charlotte's crazy weekday traffic.

It was a beautiful Sunday morning and as Carol predicted, there was little traffic on the road. We met in the parking lot first to talk for a minute. She had not told George that I was coming because she did not know what say about my abilities. Being that it was a weekend, we would have plenty of privacy. On our way up to his room, Carol expressed her uneasiness about how this would go down. I asked her to relax and trust that it would all unfold easily and effortlessly. I told her to introduce me to her dad and I would take care of the rest.

We entered the room to find George sitting up in his chair, covered with a blanket. He face lit up when he saw his beautiful daughter enter the room. He had a warm inviting smile that fit the many fond memories Carol had previously shared with me.

Carol greeted her father with a kiss and motioned for me to take a seat. She introduced me and I wasted no time initiating more conversation. Carol had told me that he had a lengthy career with the FBI so I used this to engage him.

"George, Carol tells me you were with the FBI for a number of years." He smiled and nodded. "In your experiences with them had you ever heard of the term,

Remote Viewing?" His face lit up and he shook his head yes. "Are you also familiar with the term, mental telepathy?" He shook his head again, still grinning from ear to ear. "I use mental telepathy to communicate with those that cannot speak George. Carol tells me you have been having some issues with speaking due to your Parkinson's, so we thought we would find out if you would be interested in using me to convey your needs to your daughter."

George wiggled in his chair, legs kicking up and down like an excited child might do when they could not contain their enthusiasm.

"All right George, all I need you to do is breathe as deeply as you can in order to get more oxygen to your brain, and I will do the rest. Carol will ask questions and if I feel the questions need to be reworded in order to help you clarify your needs more fully, I will do that. Are you good with this so far?" He nodded excitedly. I asked him if I could place my hands on his arm, which would help me to feel and see more deeply. He nodded in agreement. I closed my eyes and welcomed his energy into a dance with my own. His love of dance came though clearly and I conveyed what I saw to Carol. She smiled and laughed, offering that this was very true. Her father loved to dance and she had fond memories of her parents dancing. I told Carol she could begin with the questions and an hour or so later we had harvested enough information to move into the problem solving stage. I felt his energy dipping anyway, so we allowed George to drift off to sleep. Carol and I sat speaking about his feedback on the healthcare workers in charge of his daily care. Some had their own personal problems that they could not help but drag into work with them each day which emanated into George's world adding insult to injury. I took time to assess each caretaker remotely, using George's memories to connect to each person. I used great care to expound upon the issues each caretaker was having within their lives – offering some easy solutions. This helped Carol to determine what she could say in order to convey how deeply George felt for them and how wished he could make their jobs easier. He wanted nothing more than to lighten their load and tell them how much he cared for them. Carol's dissatisfaction turned to sympathy and she was so moved by the information, she stepped out of the room to speak to the caretaker in charge.

She returned to tell me that she had set up a luncheon meeting with his healthcare team the first of the week and she intended to share her father's thoughts with them.

Days later Carol called to tell me that her meeting was a huge success. The healthcare team was touched by George's comments and they wanted her to come back that afternoon to share with the next shift. The faculty and staff were able to use Carol's information to transform the way George was cared for from that day until his last.

Epilogue

THE STORIES I have shared are all true, offering a glimpse of the extraordinary experiences I have had. There are many more to come as I am now teaching crystal, indigo, rainbow and star children–or, as I affectionately call them, the Changelings—how to utilize their abilities. The first of the children's series; I Close My Eyes, My Brain Can See; is now available for children five and up. The more complete companion to *On Sacred Time:* is coming soon.

This is how I live on sacred time. I trust that you will enjoy your journey toward better health, great relationships, bringing your life's desires to fruition and finally, participating in the creation of world peace. Be well and treat others as you wish to be treated!

Nicole Myers Henderson

The Lord will guide you always;

He will satisfy your needs...and will strengthen your frame.

You will be like a well-watered garden, like a spring whose waters never fail.

Afterword

MAY 25, 2012 I began to channel information from some unknown source. The first time it happened I had just finished getting an adjustment at the chiropractors when I began to feel strange. This feeling was quite like that of an anxiety attack, but without the racing heartbeat and jitters. I managed to get to my vehicle to pull out a pen and paper when my physical hearing dimmed and my hand began to write. The words flooded my brain as if type written on a computer screen. I believe the information that came through was messages from a collection of terrestrial beings that wished to communicate their feelings about where we came from, what was happening and what was going to happen as we move forward into the future. There are three passages that came at different points in time from May 2012 through April 2013.

In the beginning, life emerged from our ancestral tides that lavished the planet. Earthen formations moved, flexing and shifting to bring forth new life and structure, revealing steadfast universal adulation for all walks of life.

No organism was dismissed nor treated with undue respect. No matter how diverse were each, all were created equal. Not one will flee from the perpetual cycle of life and death; time immemorial, changes all and none.

Today, we bare crux and veracity that what was, is, and will be shall rise once more. Terminality be not sacrificed—souls gather on all levels; commonality braves world challenges increasing adaptability.

Let it be known that we are fair and just. Reverberations of joy and sorrow are yet to come and we are distinctly affirming your oneness in order to bring about universal harmony.

Be at peace brothers and sisters. We are here to reveal your purpose throughout this sacred period. Join in community as the breaking down and rising up occurs. You are not alone.

April 25, 2013

Plagued by corrupt change the masses struggle, revealing what some might call absolute trust. Decisions made from decisions sewn provide order for those that lack the steadfast peace. You are in the midst of sacred movement. Troubles will abate, torrent affairs will be necessary. With each, a calming will come. Restitution amalgamates change. Know that you are loved and well cared for. All the old must die in order to find the newness of tomorrow. Physical casualties may be many and none. Some structures will crumble and the tall ones will topple. Eat, drink and be merry in this loving time.

Perpetuation of Life

A S I BRING my work to a close I wanted to take a look into the future to see just what was to come of humanity. I took this opportunity to speak to my God source about the perpetuation of life so that you could get a glimpse of the future as well.

God source offers:
Incremental differences support vast networks that lead to life cycles. Life cycles are affected by choices–you choose this _____ and _____ happens based on that choice. Your thoughts and actions play a vital role in the perpetuation of life.

My question: When we are each living our own sacred time, what does perpetuation of life look like over the next 50–100 years?

God source offers:
Cosmic Chasm: Structure depleted–void of known karma. Heaven on Earth, no self-limiting challenges, unity, peace, known oneness, a mind-calm or numbing takes place-quality sustainability–love abound, connected caring–purity–conscious giving.

What does the U.S. government system look like 20–50 years from today?

God source offers:
World Unified: a united front–unified in brotherhood. Headlong not headstrong

50–100 years?

God source offers:
Universal consciousness-incorporating Extraterrestrial forms–move from life sustaining to life enhancing-to being; Otherwise known as IS-ness.

Glossary

Terms found in this text

Clairvoyance: The power to perceive things that are out of insight or perceptiveness. The alleged super natural power of seeing objects or actions are moved from natural viewing.

Clairaudient: Alleged supernatural power of hearing or listening beyond that of natural hearing.

Clairsentient: Having the power of perception by the senses. The conscious mind. Characterized by sensation or feeling.

Empathy-Empath-Empathic: Identification with and understanding of another's situation, feelings and motives. The attribution to an object.

Psychic: Of or pertaining to the human mind or psyche. Of or pertaining to extraordinary, esp. extra sensory perception by or responding to such process. A medium.

Psychometry: The alleged art or faculty of divining facts concerning an object or a person associated with it, by contact with proximity to the object; (noun) divination by touching object, the alleged ability to obtain information about a person or event by touching an object related to that person or event.

Remote viewing: the act of looking at, seeing or inspecting something (a target), or an opportunity to look at or inspect something from a remote location without actually visiting to view a target in person. It is an innate skill that all human beings possess and are capable of. It is a technique easily taught, to anyone, within minutes.

Sacred: Made or declared holy. Dedicated or devoted exclusively to a single purpose, use or person. Worthy of respect, venerable of or pertaining to religious objects, rites or practices; inviolable, not to be challenged or disrespected.

Spirit: Somebody or something that is a divine, inspiring or animating influence, one of the guiding spirits, the Holy Spirit, or the life force of a person – the vital force that characterizes a human being as being alive. (I speak of Spirit in plural form because of its oneness with all other energies.)

Time: The system of sequential relationships that any event has to any other, as past, present, or future; indefinite continuous duration regarded as that which events succeed one another.

Index

R: AARP Bulletin, "How to Beat the Doctor Shortage," by Marsha Mercer (page 14), March 2013 Vol. 54 No 2

R: Kurmanalieva Ainur D., "Al-Farabi and Ibn Rushd on the Correlation Between Philosophy and Religion," Al-Farabi Kazakh National University; Equinox Publishing Ltd (2009) Bible Suite, Biblos.com 2004-2001

N: Dr. David Williams; http://www.drdavidwilliams.com/about-dr-williams/#ixzz2I9SJaJT8

N: *Natural Remedies Review*; Information and Reviews on Natural Remedies and Herbal Supplements, Pharmacist Tom Chua; http://www.natural-remedies-review.com/benefits-of-beet-juice.html

R: Taylor Richard C., "Ibn Rushd/Averroes and Islamic Rationalism," Department of Philosophy, Marquette University Milwaukee, WI, Medieval Encounters 15 (2009) 225-235

N: Encyclopedia Britannica, "Ibn Rushd (Averroes),": (1995) http://www.muslimphilosophy.com

R: Secretan Lance, "Inspirational Leadership: Destiny, Calling, and Cause" Material excerpts printed with the permission of Lance Secretan. (Oriah Mountain Dreamer, 1999)

N: "Liver Regeneration May Be Simpler Than Previously Thought",(2007, April 15) Medical News Today, http://www.medicalnewstoday.com/releases/67653.php.

N: Delecto, Ymber "Top 10 List, Health Quotes & Quotations," Inspirational-Quotes-and-Quotations.com; Sharp Business Solutions, LLC; (2007-2013): 6, http://www.inspirational-quotes-and-quotations.com/health-quotes.html

R: Gordon, Richard, "Quantum Touch: The Power to Heal," Foreword, Dr. C. Norman Shealy, M.D., Ph.D., North Atlantic Books (1999, 2002, 2006).

N: Quote by Thomas Edison; "The doctor of the future…", www.Snopes.com/quotes/edison.asp Rumor Has It. Traced to 1902–1903 from several newspapers. Snopes.com updated April 2006.

R: Kagan, Ozment & Turner "Society and Religion," Volume 1: to 1740; (2010, 2007, 2005, 2002) Pearson Education Inc; pp 272-280

R: Material excerpts from "The Guiding Philosophy for the Future of Healthcare", with permission of Nancy Gordon, Ph.D.; first published by O-Books, 2012

N: Sharif, Naubahar "Science, Technology, and Society in China I: Basic Concepts," (2013): 281, https://www.coursera.org/instructor/~281

N: Ferraro, Katie: "Nutrition for Health Promotion and Disease Prevention," The University of California, (2013) https:www.coursera.org/course/nutrition

N: Tomkin, Jonathan "Introduction to Sustainability," University of Illinois at Urbana-Champaign (2012), https://www.coursera.or/course/sustain

R: USA (2012-05-24). "Transplantation of chondrocytes utilizing a polymer-cell construct to produce tissue-engineered cartilage in the shape of a human ear"; Department of Surgery, Children's Hospital, Boston, Mass., USA; National Center for Biotechnology Information, 2012-09-14.

R: World Health Organization, "Climate change and health (reviewed November 2013): fs No266, http://www.who.int/mediacentre/factsheets/fs266/en/

R: Material excerpts from the book GOD IS NOT DEAD (c) 2008 by Amit Goswami, PhD with permission of Hampton Roads Publishing c/o Red Wheel/Weiser, LLC Newburyport MA and San Francisco, CA www.redwheelweiser.com

Wikipedia the free Encyclopedia, "Cellular Memory"; http://en.wikipedia.org/wiki/Body_memory

R: Summer Rain Mary, "Spirit Song," Hampton Roads Publishing Company Inc., (1985,1993); with permission granted by Mary Summer Rain

Biography

N ICOLE MYERS HENDERSON, known to many as a force of nature whose approaches are as certain and reliable as they are enduring. She acts from a sense of responsibility, honor and faith; possessing the will to change the world, not through bold action but through the thorough and unwavering usage of proven methods. This gifted empath utilizes techniques associated with remote viewing, advanced EFT practices, medical intuition and she created groundbreaking techniques associated within the field of Cellular Memory Detoxification therapy. Holistic consultations and instruction are available for groups as well as individuals.

Henderson, her husband Monty and three dogs currently resides in North Carolina where she founded Sage Alliance Inc. in 2001 (a non-profit 501 C 3 organization), to collaborate with professionals across the globe that educate on making better life decisions.

On Sacred Time is the first of her series of books. The first of her children's series; *I Close My Eyes*, *My Brain Can See* for children ages five and up will be available soon. Henderson's children's books are true stories pertaining to the intuitive development of her grandson Izaiah. This and others to come will ignite your spirit and assist children in living their own extraordinary life.

Endnotes

1. Estroven ® produced by Amerifit Brands, provides safe, multi-simptom menopausal relief naturally; treating symptoms of irratibility, occasional sleeplessness, energy or mood and memory issues.

2. Hylands Homeopathic Calms forte® provides temporary symptomatic relief of nervous tension and occasional sleeplessness, eases tension and promotes sleep naturally, is gentle, safe and effective

3. Bach Rescue Remedy® formulated to reduce stress. Made from flower essences; is safe, gentle and effective remedy to help restore inner calm and control.